PRESIDENTIAL ELECTION, 1872.

PROCEEDINGS

OF THE

NATIONAL UNION REPUBLICAN CONVENTION

HELD AT

Philadelphia, June 5 and 6, 1872,

WHICH NOMINATED FOR PRESIDENT AND VICE-PRESIDENT

ULYSSES S. GRANT

AND

HENRY WILSON.

REPORTED BY FRANCIS H. SMITH,
OFFICIAL REPORTER.

WASHINGTON:
GIBSON BROTHERS, PRINTERS.
1872.

NATIONAL UNION REPUBLICAN CONVENTION, 1872.

The Fifth Quadrennial Convention of the Republican Party of the United States, for the nomination of candidates for President and Vice-President, convened at the Academy of Music, in the city of Philadelphia, Wednesday, June 5th, 1872, in pursuance of the following

CALL:

The undersigned, constituting the National Committee designated by the Convention held at Chicago on the 20th of May, 1868, hereby call a Convention of the Union Republican Party at the city of Philadelphia, on Wednesday, the 5th day of June next, at 12 o'clock noon, for the purpose of nominating candidates for the offices of President and Vice-President of the United States.

Each State is authorized to be represented in the Convention by delegates equal to twice the number of Senators and Representatives to which it will be entitled in the next National Congress, and each organized Territory is authorized to send two delegates.

In calling this Convention, the Committee remind the country that the promises of the Union Republican Convention of 1868 have been fulfilled. The States lately in rebellion have been restored to their former relations to the Government. The laws of the country have been faithfully executed, public faith has been preserved, and the national credit firmly established. Governmental economy has been illustrated by the reduction, at the same time, of the public debt and of taxation; and the funding of the national debt at a lower rate of interest has been successfully inaugurated. The rights of naturalized citizens have been protected by treaties, and immigration encouraged by liberal provisions. The defenders of the Union have been gratefully remembered, and the rights and interests of labor recognized. Laws have been enacted, and are being enforced, for the protection of persons and property in all sections. Equal suffrage has been engrafted on the National Constitution; the privileges and immunities of American citizenship have become a part of the organic law, and a liberal policy has been adopted toward all who engaged in the rebellion. Complications in foreign relations have been adjusted in the interest of peace throughout the world, while the national honor has been maintained. Corruption has been exposed, offenders punished, responsibility enforced, safeguards established, and now, as heretofore, the Republican Party stands pledged to correct all abuses and carry out all reforms necessary to maintain the purity and efficiency of the public service. To continue and firmly establish its fundamental principles, we invite the co-operation of all the citizens of the United States.

WILLIAM CLAFLIN, of Massachusetts,
Chairman.

WILLIAM E. CHANDLER, of New Hampshire,
Secretary.

JOHN A. PETERS, Maine.
LUKE P. POLAND, Vermont.
L. B. FRIEZE, Rhode Island.
H. H. STARKWEATHER, Connecticut.
JAMES GOPSILL, New Jersey.
WILLIAM H. KEMBLE, Pennsylvania.
HOWARD M. JENKINS, Delaware.
B. R. COWEN, Ohio.
JOHN COBURN, Indiana.
C. B. FARWELL, Illinois.
ZACHARIAH CHANDLER, Michigan.
J. T. AVERILL, Minnesota.
DAVID ATWOOD, Wisconsin.
GEORGE W. MCCRARY, Iowa.
C. C. FULTON, Maryland.
FRANKLIN STEARNS, Virginia.
JOHN R. HUBBARD, West Virginia.
WILLIAM SLOAN, North Carolina.

THOMAS W. OSBORN, Florida.
L. C. CARPENTER, South Carolina.
JOHN H. CALDWELL, Georgia.
JAMES P. STOW, Alabama.
M. H. SOUTHWORTH, Louisiana.
A. C. FISK, Mississippi.
S. C. POMEROY, Kansas.
B. F. RICE, Arkansas.
JOHN B. CLARK, Missouri.
A. A. BURTON, Kentucky.
HORACE MAYNARD, Tennessee.
E. B. TAYLOR, Nebraska,
JAMES W. NYE, Nevada.
H. W. CORBETT, Oregon.
GEORGE C. GORHAM, California.
JOHN B CHAFFEE, Colorado.
W. A. BURLEIGH, Dakota.
SAYLES J. BOWEN, District of Columbia.

WASHINGTON, D. C., *January* 11, 1872.

WEDNESDAY, JUNE 5, 1872.

THE CONVENTION CALLED TO ORDER.

At 12 o'clock noon, Hon. WILLIAM CLAFLIN, of Massachusetts, Chairman of the National Committee, called the Convention to order, and spoke as follows:

SPEECH OF GOVERNOR CLAFLIN.

Gentlemen of the Convention : Elected according to the usages of the Republican Party, in conventions of the people held in every State, you have assembled for the purpose of placing in nomination candidates for the two highest offices in the gift of the American people. You represent a party founded on the broadest principles of freedom, justice, and humanity, and whose achievements have been the wonder and admiration of the civilized world. The promises of reform and progress made four years ago have been faithfully fulfilled [applause] in the guarantee by the nation of equal rights to all; in the reduction of the public expenditures and the public debt; in the decrease of the public burdens; in the improvement of the public credit; in the establishment of the public faith that no act of repudiation shall ever stain the statute-book, and in securing peace and order throughout the entire Republic.

You are summoned to declare anew your fidelity to those principles and purposes which have brought such beneficent results to the nation. We will not fear that the people will desert those who have been faithful to their high trust, for other men and other organizations, although they may adopt our principles and promise to adhere to our policy. Let us go forward with confident faith that our cause will triumph, notwithstanding unexpected defections, over all combinations, however skilfully planned, because in its continued success are centred the best interests and the highest hopes of the country. [Cheers.]

Before proceeding further, I will invite the Rev. Dr. Reed to lead the Convention in prayer.

The Rev. Dr. ALEXANDER REED, of the Central Presbyterian Church, of Philadelphia, then offered the following prayer:

PRAYER.

Our Father in Heaven! we bow before Thee at Thy throne. In infinite mercy listen to our prayer. Thou art the eternal God, the self-existent and unchangeable Creator. Immensity Thy dwelling-place, the Universe Thy home, greater than all Thy works, and worthy of the reverence and homage and love of all Thy creatures, Thou only art the Lord, exalted, supreme. There is no counsellor for Thee; for with Thee there are no mysteries and Thou makest no mistakes. Thou sittest on the circle of the heavens; all its inhabitants are but as grasshoppers. Nations are before Thee but as dust in the balances; yet, though Thou art so exalted, Thy very greatness brings Thee near to us, for Thy spirit and presence fill heaven and earth; Thou dost encompass every creature Thou hast made, and in all heights and depths, throughout all space, boundless, infinite, Thou art God over all, blessed forever. We praise Thee. We rejoice to know Thee as our Creator, King, and Father; and in the name of our ascended Saviour we come into Thy presence at this august hour seeking grace, Thy favor. We, pleading Thy promises to be nigh unto all that call upon Thee in truth, that they who ask shall receive of Thee, come humbly unto Thee, yet confidently, believing that Thou art the hearer of prayer.

Our Father, bless us to-day. Bless our beloved country with abundant and abiding benedictions. Our experience of Thy loving care through all the past gives us confidence to seek Thy guarding, guiding Providence for the future. Oh, God! for all that Thou hast done for us a nation, thereof we are glad.

In the travail pains of birth, through feeble infancy, and in dark and dangerous days of division and strife, Thou hast preserved us. Oh, bless us still. Through almost a century Thou hast never failed us; keep us still; leave us not to ourselves, to self-confidence, to pride, to forgetfulness of God. We do thank Thee for Thy favor and Thy faithfulness, for Thy patience and paternal love. We thank Thee that Thou hast proclaimed liberty throughout all the land unto all the inhabitants thereof; that Thou hast broken the bondsmen's fetters, and said to the oppressed, Go Free. We thank Thee that Thou hast ordained peace for us and prosperity in all our borders. We thank Thee for our new birth of freedom, and we pray Thee to guide and keep us, that this "Government of the people, by the people, and for the people, shall not perish from the earth." Therefore, bless Thy servant, the President of these United States, and guide him in all his diversified duties by Thy hand. Bless his counsellors, each and all. Bless the Governor of this Commonwealth, and of every Commonwealth throughout the land. Bless every citizen, old and young, high and low. Bless the noble soldiery that still survive the days of blood and fire. May these noble heroes realize the gratitude of a rescued people and the care of a loving God. And now, O God! most high and holy, we devoutly pray do Thou bless this vast National Convention, gathered hither from North and South, and East and West, to transact business for a mighty constituency. May Thy blessing be upon them. May these leaders of the people and of a party be led by Thee. May these wise counsellors seek and receive that wisdom that cometh down from above, which is profitable to direct. Do Thou, Ruler Divine, preside over these deliberations, and may all questions issued and concluded here be acceptable to Thee, and whatever men may intend, do Thou superintend so that Thou shall be glorified, and the highest and holiest interests of this land may be secured and perpetuated. Guide these, Thy servants, to such selections of leaders as shall meet the approval of the good and patriotic throughout this great Republic, and shall be approved by Thee. And may this noble party now represented here—a party of glorious history and immortal renown—be wisely guided of God to such a policy as shall prove it in the future, as in the past, favored of Thee. And be pleased, Thou God of nations, to speak to this people gathered from all peoples, and make it a nation willing to obey and love Thee. And most devoutly do we pray that Thou wilt, amid the kingdoms of this world, advance Thy kingdom, blessed God! Remember the family of mankind; bring us all into one blood-beat again. May we feel heart to heart the world around, and in the same electric connection of love may the whole earth experience at last the consolation of Thy redemptive power, and stand disenthralled and united before God, a blessed brotherhood, baptized into purity; and then at last may there break forth, accordant with the choral utterances of heaven, a voice of joy the world around, giving praise unto the Father, Son, and Holy Ghost.

And now we commit ourselves and all our work to Thee. Bless us individually, we implore. As we here seek to exalt a ruler over this Republic, may we not forget to seek to exalt Thee ruler over our hearts and lives, as men—as mortal, as immortal men. And all we ask and all we offer is in the name of Him who taught us when we pray to say: Our Father which art in Heaven. Hallowed be Thy name. Thy kingdom come. Thy will be done in earth as it is in Heaven. Give us this day our daily bread. And forgive us our trespasses, as we forgive those that trespass against us. And lead us not into temptation, but deliver us from evil. For thine is the kingdom, and the power, and the glory, forever. Amen.

TEMPORARY CHAIRMAN.

Governor CLAFLIN resumed:

Gentlemen of the Convention: I have the pleasure, by the instruction of the National Committee, of presenting to you the Hon. MORTON MCMICHAEL, of Philadelphia, for temporary Chairman. [Great applause.] Those of you who favor that nomination will say *aye.*

The nomination was unanimously confirmed.

Hon. HENRY S. LANE, of Indiana; Hon. JAMES H. PLATT, JR., of Virginia, and Hon. JAMES LEWIS, of Louisiana, having been appointed by the Chairman for that purpose, escorted Mr. MCMICHAEL to the Chair. On reaching the platform he was greeted with enthusiastic and prolonged applause, and, being presented by Governor CLAFLIN to the Convention, he spoke as follows:

ADDRESS OF THE TEMPORARY CHAIRMAN.

Gentlemen of the Convention: I thank you for the privilege of presiding, even for the brief period I shall enjoy that honor, over such an assemblage as this. I am the more gratified because as a delegate from Pennsylvania, and a resident of Philadelphia, it gives me an occasion to welcome you to our State and City, [applause;] to say to you all how glad we are to have you among us; to express to you our intention to promote your comfort while you remain with us; and our desire that when you leave us you will leave with such impressions as will induce you frequently to return. Under any circumstances, it would be a source of satisfaction to us to have the presence of so many distinguished men, gathered from all parts of this mighty land, which grows and stretches so rapidly that in these recurring quadrennial convocations new States, new Territories, and in this case, happily for the cause of humanity and progress, a new race—[great applause]—new, at least, in the possession of political rights and civil functions, and soon to be endowed with all the attributes of equality —are represented; under any circumstances your presence would be to us a source of satisfaction, and it is especially so in view of the purpose which has brought you hither. The malcontents who recently met at Cincinnati were without a constituency; the Democrats who are soon to meet at Baltimore will be without a principle. [Hearty applause.] The former, having no motive in common but personal disappointment, attempted a fusion of repelling elements, which has resulted in explosion; the latter, degraded from the high estate they once occupied, propose an abandonment of their identity, which means death. Unlike the first, you are the authentic exponents of a great national organization, based upon principles

> Firm as the marble, founded as the rock;
> As broad and general as the casing air:

[cheers,] unlike the last, your object is to preserve, not to destroy. And, gentlemen, differing from both these in character and aims, you will differ no less in the nature of your deliberations. On the subject which has most perplexed, and must continue to perplex their councils, in yours, rather let me say in ours, there will be absolute harmony. With us the selection of a Presidential candidate is a foregone conclusion. In that regard the people have decided for us in advance, and we have only to put

their will into proper shape by formally nominating Ulysses S. Grant. [Enthusiastic and continued cheering, the whole audience rising to their feet.] And with the blessing of God we shall not only make that nomination without demur, without debate, without dissent, but we shall make it under such auspices as will insure its complete and abundant ratification at the polls. [Applause.]

It does not need, nor, considering my temporary occupation of this chair, would it be suitable that I should enter into any elaborate commentary as to the merits of our candidate. But this I will say, that notwithstanding all the malignant venom that has been spit at him; all the odious calumnies that have been heaped upon him; all the disgraceful slanders that have been circulated in regard to him, General Grant at this moment enjoys more of the confidence of his countrymen, is believed by them to be an honester, truer, and better man than any of his detractors. [Great applause and cries of assent.] No one in our day has been more causelessly, more shamelessly villified; no one will be more thoroughly vindicated. The great heart of the American people beats responsively to truth and justice, and as they have tried and tested and trust him; as they know that his administration has been wise and faithful; as they have seen the nation prosper under his rule as it has never before prospered, they will stand by and defend, and, when the ballot-box gives them a chance to do so, avenge him. [Cheers, and cries of "They will."] Remembering the sore trials which, along with his fellow-soldiers, he underwent during the war, his sacrifices of ease and comfort, his perils by day and by night, the exposure by means of which those who now revile him were able to secure luxurious repose at a safe distance from danger, they are quite willing that he should indulge in "palace cars and cigars and seaside loiterings," [cheers and laughter;] and they mean to furnish him with the opportunity of enjoying these for at least four years to come.

As to the Vice-Presidency, no doubt, gentlemen, there will be various preferences. Some of us will at first favor one, some another, but we shall all strive to obtain the best man; and when the choice is ultimately made I trust we shall all feel that we have succeeded. [Applause.] In regard to the platform to be adopted it is not for me to anticipate; but along with other important doctrines it will undoubtedly contain the widest recognition of human freedom, and the clearest affirmation of the duties which the Government owes to its laboring masses, wherever and however employed, in town or country; and with such candidates and such a creed, whether we have to encounter the decaying remnants of a once powerful party, but now so feeble that it is crying piteously to its enemy for succor; or an incongruous alliance of ill-assorted factions, with no band of union but the greed of office; or all of them combined, we shall go forth conquering and to conquer. [Hearty and continued applause.]

Music by the Band.

TEMPORARY SECRETARIES.

The CHAIRMAN. The Convention will now proceed to indicate persons to be selected as Secretaries of this temporary organization.

On motion of Mr. STANLEY T. PULLEN, of Maine, the following-named persons were elected as temporary Secretaries of the Convention:

JOHN W. NEWLIN, of New Jersey.
HIRAM POTTER, Jr., of Florida.
JOHN R. HUBBARD, of West Virginia.

COMMITTEE ON CREDENTIALS.

The CHAIRMAN. It is customary at this stage of the proceedings for the delegates from the different States and Territories to designate one member of their number for the Committee on Credentials. The Secretary will call the roll of the States, and as it is called some gentleman representing each of them will indicate its choice in the matter to which I have referred.

The roll of the States was then called, and the following names were announced:

Alabama	J. W. Burke.	New York	Edward W. Foster.
Arkansas	J. H. Johnson.	North Carolina	Lewis Hilliard.
California	Thomas Fallon.	Ohio	Griffith Ellis.
Connecticut	James D. Frary.	Oregon	Hiram Smith.
Delaware	Benjamin Burton.	Pennsylvania	L. D. Shoemaker.
Florida	J. H. Armstrong.	Rhode Island	Edward L. Freeman.
Georgia	Edwin Belcher.	South Carolina	S. A. Swails.
Illinois	J. F. Alexander.	Tennessee	R. R. Butler.
Indiana	M. L. Bundy.	Texas	W. A. Sayler.
Iowa	Isaac Pendleton.	Vermont	George W. Grandey.
Kansas	William Baldwin.	Virginia	Robert Norton.
Kentucky	Samuel L. Casey.	West Virginia	George Edwards.
Louisiana	Mortimer F. Smith.	Wisconsin	Joseph G. Thorpe.
Maine	John E. Butler.	Arizona	John Titus.
Maryland	Alexander Randall.	Colorado	Jerome B. Chaffee.
Massachusetts	E. B. Stoddard.	Dakota	(Contested.)
Michigan	James H. Stone.	District of Columbia	John F. Cooke.
Minnesota	C. H. Goodsell.	Idaho	E. J. Curtis.
Mississippi	Edwin Hill.	Montana	Lucius B. Church.
Missouri	George A. Moser.	New Mexico	William Breeden.
Nebraska	John Roberts.	Utah	(Contested.)
Nevada	C. C. Stevenson.	Washington	E. Dorfield.
New Hampshire	Dexter Richards.	Wyoming	John W. Donnellan.
New Jersey	George Wurts.		

When Utah and Dakota were called, announcements were made by delegates from those Territories that, as there were contesting delegations, they would make no nominations for this committee.

COMMITTEE ON PERMANENT ORGANIZATION.

The CHAIRMAN. The Secretary will now proceed to call the roll of States, in order that the delegation from each State may suggest one of their number as a member of the Committee on Permanent Organization.

Mr. J. L. KECK, of Ohio. *Mr. Chairman:* In order to save time, I move that when the Secretary calls the roll, each State shall name the members whom it desires to have placed on the Committee on Permanent Organization, the Committee on Resolutions, and the Committee on Rules and Orders.

The motion was lost.

The CHAIRMAN. The committee now to be elected is the Committee on Permanent Organization.

A DELEGATE. Are we expected to present the name of one man for one committee, or the names of the committee for all?

The CHAIRMAN. Just one man from each State on Permanent Organization.

A DELEGATE. Call the Territories.

The CHAIRMAN. It is not customary to call the Territories. If it is the desire of the Convention, however, it shall be done.

On motion, it was voted that the Territories and the District of Columbia be allowed representation on all the permanent committees.

A MEMBER OF THE COMMITTEE ON CREDENTIALS. *Mr. Chairman:* I ask leave for the Committee on Credentials to retire to Horticultural Hall.

Leave was granted.

The Secretary then proceeded with the calling of the roll for Committee on Permanent Organization, with the following result:

Alabama.......................Isaac Heyman.
Arkansas......................J. M. Johnson.
California....................F. K. Shattuck.
Connecticut...................Bartlett Bent.
Delaware......................John C. Clark.
Florida.......................F. N. Wicker.
Georgia.......................Jefferson F. Long.
Illinois......................Enoch Emery.
Indiana.......................George K. Steele.
Iowa..........................A. R. Anderson.
Kansas........................Josiah Kellogg.
Kentucky......................John B. Bruner.
Louisiana.....................E. W. Robinson.
Maine.........................Hiram Bliss, Jr.
Maryland......................John T. Ensor.
Massachusetts.................Sylvander Johnson.
Michigan......................James Birney.
Minnesota.....................A. E. Rice.
Mississippi...................A. K. Davis.
Missouri......................E. O. Stanard.
Nebraska......................John D. Neligh.
Nevada........................George M. Sabin.
New Hampshire.................Daniel Barnard.
New Jersey....................Levi D. Jarrard.
New York......................John N. Hungerford.
North Carolina................James H. Harris.
Ohio..........................N. H. Van Vorhes.
Oregon........................Myer Hirsch.
Pennsylvania..................Charles Albright.
Rhode Island..................William D. Brayton.
South Carolina................W. B. Nash.
Tennessee.....................William Y. Elliott.
Texas.........................W. A. Ellett.
Vermont.......................George Wilkins.
Virginia......................John A. Harman.
West Virginia.................John E. Schley.
Wisconsin.....................Thaddeus C. Pound.
Arizona.......................James H. Toole.
Colorado......................George M. Chillicothe.
Dakota........................(No nomination.)
District of Columbia..Alex. R. Shepherd.
Idaho.........................E. C. Ford.
Montana.......................L. B. Church.
New Mexico....................(No nomination.)
Utah..........................(No nomination.)
Washington....................(No nomination.)
Wyoming.......................George W. Corey.

A MEMBER OF COMMITTEE ON PERMANENT ORGANIZATION. *Mr. Chairman:* I ask leave for the Committee on Permanent Organization to retire.

The CHAIRMAN. The Committee on Permanent Organization will please retire. Rooms are provided in Horticultural Hall, and the Committee of Arrangements will escort them there.

A DELEGATE. *Mr. Chairman:* I move that the election of the Committee on Resolutions be deferred till the report of the Committee on Permanent Organization be received.

The motion was lost.

Mr. JOHN R. POPHAM, of Virginia. *Mr. Chairman:* I move that when the roll of States be called for the Committee on Resolutions, the chairmen of the several delegations report the names of the persons that have been selected for the two remaining committees—the Committee on Resolutions and on Rules.

The motion was agreed to, and the Secretary proceeded to call the roll of States, with the following result:

COMMITTEE ON RESOLUTIONS.

Alabama.......................R. M. Reynolds.
Arkansas......................William H. Grey.
California....................J. H. Withington.
Connecticut...................Joseph R. Hawley.
Delaware......................Henry F. Pickels.
Florida.......................J. W. Johnson.
Georgia.......................Dawson A. Walker.
Illinois......................Herman Raster.
Indiana.......................Charles Cruft.
Iowa..........................William Vandever.
Kansas........................C. A. Morris.
Kentucky......................James Speed.
Louisiana.....................John Ray.
Maine.........................S. T. Pullen.
Maryland......................Thomas A. Spence.
Massachusetts.................J. B. D. Cogswell.
Michigan......................William A. Howard.
Minnesota.....................W. E. Hicks.
Mississippi...................John R. Lynch.
Missouri......................J. H. Stover.
Nebraska......................J. B. Weston.
Nevada........................L. H. Head.
New Hampshire.................Ossian Ray.
New Jersey....................Charles Hewitt.
New York......................James N. Matthews.
North Carolina................James W. Hood.
Ohio..........................R. B. Hayes.
Oregon........................H. R. Kincaid.
Pennsylvania..................Glenni W. Scofield.
Rhode Island..................William Goddard.

COMMITTEE ON RESOLUTIONS—*continued.*

South Carolina..........Robert B. Elliott.
Tennessee...................A. J. Ricks.
Texas.............. ....J. W. Talbot.
Vermont...............Benjamin H. Steele.
Virginia...................Edward Daniels.
West Virginia............Thomas B. Swann.
Wisconsin..................Thomas S. Allen.
Arizona.....................(No nomination.)
Colorado..................Jerome B. Chaffee.

Dakota ....(No nomination.)
District of Columbia...Alex. R. Shepherd.
Idaho...............................E. J. Curtis.
Montana........................W. F. Sanders.
New Mexico................(No nomination.)
Utah...........................(No nomination.)
Washington...............(No nomination.)
Wyoming..............John W. Donnellan.

COMMITTEE ON RULES AND ORDER OF BUSINESS.

Alabama..........................W. B. Jones.
Arkansas....................Stephen Wheeler.
California............Charles M. Patterson.
Connecticut...............Daniel Chadwick.
Delaware.............Charles F. Richards.
Florida.........................John W. Butler.
Georgia....................James M. Simms.
Illinois.........................Israel A. Powell.
Indiana....................C. W. Chapman.
Iowa.................................I. W. Card.
Kansas...........................H. C. Cross.
Kentucky..............William H. Gibson.
Louisiana......................W. G. Elliott.
Maine.........................A. H. S. Davis.
Maryland.........Samuel M. Shoemaker.
Massachusetts..................Oliver Ames.
Michigan.....................George Willard.
Minnesota...... ....R. F. Crowell.
Mississippi........................A. Parker.
Missouri......................John C. Orrick.
Nebraska...................H. M. Atkinson.
Nevada...................George M. Sabin.
New Hampshire.............J. W. Johnson.
New Jersey.................David Vickers.

New York...............B. Platt Carpenter.
North Carolina.........George H. Brown.
Ohio.............................W. C. Cooper.
Oregon.............................J. F. Devore.
Pennsylvania................C. W. Gilfillan.
Rhode Island..........Latimer W. Ballou.
South Carolina........Thomas J. Mackey.
Tennessee.............George E. Grisham.
Texas..................James P. Newcomb.
Vermont...........James Hutchinson, Jr.
Virginia.........................G. G. Goddell.
West Virginia........D. D. T. Farnsworth.
Wisconsin..................C. J. L. Meyer.
Arizona....................(No nomination.)
Colorado............George M. Chillicothe.
Dakota.......................(No nomination.)
District of Columbia.......John F. Cooke.
Idaho...............................B. J. Curtis.
Montana......................L. B. Church.
New Mexico................(No nomination.)
Utah..........................(No nomination.)
Washington...............(No nomination.)
Wyoming..................George W. Corey.

General JOHN A. LOGAN, in response to repeated and continued calls, came upon the platform, and having been introduced by the Chairman, spoke as follows:

REMARKS OF SENATOR LOGAN.

Gentlemen of the Convention: There is nothing that would delight me more, if I were capable of doing so, than to entertain you with a speech. I know I ought not to judge, but if you will allow me to be the judge on this occasion, I will suggest that I do not think that this is the time, so far as I am concerned. I am so out of voice from an effort last night that I am physically unable to address you at any great length, nor do I think it would be proper for me to attempt it.

There are a great many gentlemen here whom I know you are anxious to hear; men who are able, men who are eloquent, and men whom you have not heard before.

A DELEGATE. We want to hear a few words from Logan. [Applause.]

Senator LOGAN, (resuming.) I will only say then, for I very certainly cannot attempt to detain you with a speech, that if the people of this whole land to-day could see this convention assembled, its appearance and the manifestations of enthusiasm at the mention of the name of the man whom you intend to present to the American people to be voted for for President, [great applause.] it would gladden the national heart. I am proud, and I am glad to know, that to-day, after four years' trial of the President of the United States, when you come here to Philadelphia to repeat what you did four years ago—his nomination—there exists more enthusiasm in the midst of the delegates, four to one, than we found when we first presented him to the American people. [Applause.]

This only proves the fact that he has done well. He has performed the duty that you imposed upon him to your entire satisfaction. [Applause.] And you come here to repeat, "Well done, thou good and faithful servant. Thou hast been faithful over a few things, we will make thee ruler over many things." [Great applause.]

After the remarks of General LOGAN, continued calls were made from the audience for "Morton," "Banks," and others.

Mr. CHARLES S. SPENCER, of New York. *Mr. Chairman:* The delegation from the State of New York desire me to move that their venerable head, the oldest pioneer in the cause of emancipation in this room, [cheers,] GERRITT SMITH, [great cheering,] be invited to address you.

The motion was received with great enthusiasm, delegates all over the building rising in their places, waving their hats and handkerchiefs, and calling for Mr. SMITH.

The venerable gentleman rose in his place and bowed repeatedly, the assemblage continuing to cheer him. The Chairman came down from his platform and moved towards the part of the house where Mr. SMITH was, waiting to conduct him before the audience. Music being called for to fill up the gap until Mr. SMITH could get upon the stage, the band in the circle played "Hail to the Chief."

When the music ceased, Mr. Smith stood before the cheering assemblage.

The CHAIRMAN. Now, gentlemen of the Convention, three rousing cheers!

Three cheers were given with a hearty will; and Mr. SMITH spoke as follows:

REMARKS OF GERRITT SMITH.

Gentlemen of the Convention: I will detain you but a few minutes, for I fear I shall not be heard distinctly from my hoarseness. Gentlemen, the time has nearly come round again when the American people are to choose their Chief Magistrate. Who shall it be? [Cries of "Grant!" "Grant!" and loud cheers.] Whom shall we nominate? [Renewed cries for Grant.] You all say Grant; well, I agree with you. Why do we all say Grant? Because he was the savior of the country. [Applause.] Because he has blessed his country in time of peace. [Applause.]

From the breaking out of the rebellion the American people defended their country bravely, but not always successfully. They passed through a long alternation of successes and defeats, and quite as many defeats as successes. Sunshine was now upon their cause and now it was wrapped in gloom. It was in this crisis, in this period of fear, that General Grant was called to the head of the army.

The people had begun to despair of ultimate success, when General Grant, by the persistency of his policy, by his resolve to fight it out on the same line if it took all summer, achieved victory.

This course subjected him to much severe criticism on the part of distinguished gentlemen; but the final battle was fought and won; Lee surrendered, and our country, then divided, became one again.

I said that he had helped us in time of peace, also. He has done so. He has preserved us on terms of amity with all the nations of the earth. He has preserved the policy of kindness towards the poor, erring, deluded Indians.

And he is doing what he can, and if you give him time he will fully accomplish it, to crush out Ku-Kluxism and save the negro and the few white men who defend the negro from the bloody, fearful, and terrible vengeance threatened against them.

But it is said that General Grant has had one term of the Presidency, and now he ought to retire to give place to another. Well, my friends, my doctrine is that his having proved himself a good President once, proves him fitted for it a second term. [Applause.]

This was the doctrine of the American people when they re-elected Washington, the first savior of the country. [Applause.] It was their doctrine when they re-elected Lincoln, the second savior of his country. [More applause.] It is their doctrine in regard to the third savior of the country, and they will re-elect General Grant accordingly. [Wild applause.]

It is said, too, that Grant has made mistakes. Oh, yes; he has. All Presidents make mistakes. To err is human—human in the broadest sense. Not even Presidents are exempt from liabilities to mistakes. It is said that some of his appointments have turned out badly. Yes; some of the appointments of all Presidents turn out badly. They are not all gifted with clairvoyance. They don't all read character in advance, [laughter,] but we find ample consolation in this fact, that notwithstanding the industrious efforts—and as venomous as industrious—to bring home to him corruption in these appointments, to foist upon him money-making or other corrupt motives, all this has signally failed. [Great enthusiasm.]

Now, we want Grant, I say, a few years longer in the Presidency. He is doing well. He is crushing out Ku-Kluxism, and if the Government allow him power enough he will make a complete end of it. We want his leadership a few years longer until we shall reach full and final triumph in this matter. [Applause.]

And, now, finally, we must have Grant a few years longer in the Presidency, because the anti-slavery battle is not yet fought out. This is with me the point of interest. I care comparatively little for dollars and cents; I go for human rights. [Applause.] I say it is not yet fought out, and it will not be fought out so long as a single shred of Ku-Kluxism exists in the land. It will not be fought out so long as a single man in this land is deprived of one single solitary right on account of his color. [Intense enthusiasm.] I cannot but feel, whenever I see in the proceedings of Congress a defeat of a Ku-Klux bill or of a Civil Rights bill, that these are steps toward the revival of American slavery.

We want Grant, therefore, for four years more, until we shall see the end of these diabolical outrages, and until the right shall finally and fully triumph in this country. [Applause.]

Loud and persistent calls for "Morton!" now followed, and at length Senator O. P. MORTON, of Indiana, was assisted to the platform. He was greeted with much cheering and enthusiasm, and on being seated, for an infirmity prevents his standing, was presented to the audience as follows:

The CHAIRMAN. There, gentlemen, there is our great advocate, Governor MORTON. [Applause.]

SPEECH OF SENATOR MORTON.

Gentlemen of the Convention: In the enthusiasm which prevails here to-day I see the unmistakable evidence of victory in November. This enthusiasm is not manufactured; it is spontaneous, it comes from the hearts of this audience here to-day, representing the great mass of the people of the United States. [Applause.] You represent the Republican party, and that party has a great mission to perform, a mission that is no less than taking care of this country. To that party the interests of this great nation must be committed in the future, as they have been preserved and fostered by it in the past. The Republican party is not a worshipper of men. We hold fast to principles rather than to men. We stand by the pioneers of Republican principles. We do them all honor, but only so long as they remain faithful to those principles. [Applause.] When a pioneer falls, he falls farther than anybody else. [Cries of "Good!" and applause.] Among several nations of antiquity the idea prevailed that the father had a right to kill his own offspring, and some men who think they were the fathers of the Republican party have recently set up the claim that on that account they have the right to kill it. [Laughter and applause.] As a general thing we deny the paternity. [Applause.] But if we admitted the paternity we should deny the right to kill. What are the things that the Republican party yet have to do? I know it has been dinned in our ears for two or three years past that our mission was performed. Whenever a man has been beaten for the nomination for Congress, he has generally come to the conclusion that the mission of the Republican party was at an end, and we ought to form a new party. If he has been turned out of office for malfeasance, or if he has failed to get into office, he concluded that the duties of the Republican party are at an end, and that a new organization ought to be formed. [Applause.]

I ask you to-day, what are the duties before us? First, in regard to those questions which concern the administration. It is the duty of the Republican party to perfect our national financial system; [cheers] gradually but surely, not by violence, or spasmodic efforts, to bring our currency to par. We are certainly and safely approaching that event. We do not propose to accomplish it by violent action, but by using the natural causes which are now at work, we shall place the credit of the nation upon a higher basis than it ever occupied before, and upon a higher basis than that occupied by the credit of any other nation. [Applause.] We shall do this by faithfully performing all our promises; by keeping our contracts in the spirit and the letter; and by the gradual but certain reduction of the public debt. [Cheers.]

While we shall carry out to the letter the present policy we have on hand, while we have nothing new on the subject, (and I may say in regard to platforms that it is scarcely necessary for this Convention to adopt one, for the platform of the Republican party is found in its history for the last ten years, and it is to be found in the present policy of the Administration)—I say, while we shall do this, it is for us to carry out and consecrate the reforms upon which this Administration has already entered, [cheers,] for our work is not done in regard to those great measures which have grown out of the war.

It is for the Republican party to establish the fourteenth and fifteenth amendments, [cheers;] to plant them in the Constitution, beyond peradventure, so that they shall be recognized by all parties; so that there shall no longer be any considerable party in this country which shall dare to question the legality or the validity of these amendments. [Applause.] It is for the Republican party to establish fully the rights of the colored men of this country. [Applause.] Our work will not be done until they shall be conceded by all parties, and they shall have the full and free enjoyment of their rights in every portion of this country. [Applause.] Until they shall be in the full enjoyment not only of all their political but of all their civil rights. Our work will not be done until there shall be equal protection under the law extended to men of every race and color, and to all men of all political views in every part of the United States. [Applause.] The mission of the Republican party will not be performed as long as there shall remain a Ku-Klux organization in any State of this Union, [applause,] for that organization but sleeps in some of the States, and it will awake to active, terrible life, shortly before the Presidential election, if there shall not be proper legislation, if there shall not be a firm, bold administration of the Government which shall afford protection to all. [Cheers.]

Our Government protects the rights of American citizens everywhere, in every foreign country. If half a dozen Americans were murdered in London or Havana, by a mob, we should demand the prompt punishment of the murderers. It would be a cause of national offence, if the Government of England or Spain did not use every exertion to bring the murderers to punishment. The murder of an American citizen in a foreign land requires the immediate notice of the Government, and his rights must be vindicated, if need be, by the whole power of the nation. Shall it, then, be said that the Government has the power and the right to protect American citizens in every country but our own? [Cheers.]

I hold that when any State fails, refuses, or, from any cause, is unable to secure to her citizens the equal protection of the laws, security for life, liberty, and property—I hold that it is within the power and is the absolute and solemn duty of the Government of the United States to extend protection in such cases. [Applause.]

In passing what is called the Ku-Klux law, we did not intend to place an arbitrary power in the hands of the President of the United States, to be exercised by caprice or for selfish or partisan purposes. That power was placed there for the purpose of protecting, or enabling him to protect, the lives, liberty, and property of hundreds and thousands, and even of millions of people in some of the Southern States, where the State governments had been unable or had failed to grant such protection.

We knew, when placing that power in the hands of the President, he would not abuse it. He has not abused it. [Great applause.] And whatever may have been said, allow me to say here that the Ku-Klux law has done more good in a shorter time than any law ever enacted by the Congress of the United States. It has operated like a charm. It has protected thousands and thousands of people from murder, from outrage, and from exile. And those in the South who denounce that law, and who oppose the re-enactment for another year of the power to the President to suspend the writ of *habeas corpus* in case of revolution or rebellion, do not oppose it because any wrong has been done, because any rights have been violated, but they oppose it because they are unwilling that a certain instrumentality shall be crushed out, which, being left uncontrolled, may control, may absolutely sway, the political action of certain States of this Union. We desire only fair and honest elections. We want men of all parties and of all colors, without regard to previous condition, to have perfect liberty in the exercise of their political rights. [Applause.] And it is because they have not been accorded heretofore that that law was enacted.

Fellow-citizens, I believe that the salvation of this country, I believe that our greatest and best interests, are bound up with the continued predominance of the Republican party for years to come. [Applause.] I am not an advocate of the Republican party merely as a partisan, but because it has been the great instrumentality by which this country has been saved in the past, and by which, in my judgment, it must be preserved in the future. [Applause.] In a Government like ours there are, there must be, parties. Men entertaining similar principles must act together; they cannot act together without organization and co-operation, and that makes a party. When you have broken this party down, what security will you have that you can ever get another which will carry out and consummate its work? Stand fast by principle. Look to the future, and be guided by the light of the past. Sometimes a great light is extinguished; sometimes one of those to whom the people have been accustomed to look up falls by the wayside. We may drop a tear of regret, but we should not pause. [Applause.] Remember that the Republican party is greater than any man. It is much greater than all its leaders combined. But among the greatest of our statesmen and politicians a great many errors are committed. It is said that General Grant has committed his errors. I do not deny it; but I am happy to say that most of them are trivial. They do not go to the essence and substance of his administration, and some of those who now oppose him have committed a greater error. Any man who supposes that he has strength enough to break up the Republican party will commit a very grave blunder [Applause.] Any man who supposes he can lead the Republican party into the ranks of the Democratic party, by means of any back door or back stairs, for the sake of plunder, commits a very great blunder. [Applause and laughter.]

Several men who have been distinguished in the Republican party, whom we have been looking up to as leaders and pioneers, have committed this mistake; but when they have made this mistake they have been dropped and passed away forever, and there has been no perceptible influence produced upon the party. [Applause.] A pebble dropped into a pool produces a ripple for a little while, but it very soon becomes placid; you cannot tell by looking at the surface of the pool what has happened. So, the greatest man in the Republican party, if he shall be unfaithful to its principles; if, by reason of personal disappointment or irritation he shall still endeavor to destroy its organization, or betray it into the hands of its enemies, he will sink out of sight, to disturb the surface of the political world as little as the pebble when dropped into the lake. [Applause.]

Then stand fast by your principles. You will on to-morrow nominate General Grant. [Applause.] General Grant has told the American people that he had no policy to urge against their wishes and their understandings. He has made pledges which have been faithfully redeemed. He endeavors to carry out the national wish whenever he finds out what that wish is. The judgment of all men is better than the judgment of any one man. The common sense of the country is better than the judgment of any man, however lofty or angelic may be his abilities, and the faithful public servant endeavors to find out what is the popular will, what is the wish of the nation, and then to carry it out, understanding that the great object of government is to subserve and carry out the wishes of the nation rather than to carry out the policy or theory of any individual. General Grant's career has been a great success in all essential and substantial matters. It has been a continual triumph.

He has fostered and protected the interests of the people. I believe they are intelligent enough to understand it, and that they intend to entrust those interests to him for four more years. [Applause.] But whenever General Grant shall betray the principles of the Republican party upon which he was elected, whenever he shall become recreant to his high duties, he will pass away as some other men have passed away. He will be condemned by the popular breath as other men are condemned. [Applause.]

After Senator MORTON had concluded, calls for several gentlemen were made, and quieted by the Chairman, who announced that a delegate from Massachusetts had the floor.

Mr. GEORGE B. LORING, of Massachusetts. *Mr. President and Gentlemen:* I do not propose to make a speech. I understand that the Committee on Permanent Organization are ready to report, or will be in a moment. It has been usual when there has been any conflict in regard to the delegates in the conventions, that the Committee on Permanent Organization should not report until the Committee on Credentials have made their report. But there is no difficulty whatever. The Committee on Credentials have a mere formality to go through, and as the Committee on Permanent Organization is now nearly ready to report, I move they be requested to do so at the earliest practicable moment.

The motion was agreed to.

Mr. A. J. RANSIER, of South Carolina. Mr. President, we have listened with great pleasure to the eloquent and expressive words which have fallen from the sage, and if I may so express it, the philosopher of New York—I allude to Mr. Gerritt Smith; and as the time and occasion seem auspicious, I ask on behalf of this delegation that the Convention now listen to Governor James L. Orr, of South Carolina. [Cries all over the house of "Orr!" "Orr!" and great cheering.]

Governor ORR, upon appearing on the stage, was received with great cheers. He spoke as follows:

SPEECH OF HON. JAMES L. ORR.

Gentlemen of the Convention: I feel that the call which has been made with so much enthusiasm by this body is more of a compliment to the section from which I come than any personal compliment intended for me. [Cries of "No!" "No!"] We are here for the purpose of nominating candidates for the Presidency and Vice-Presidency of the United States, for the Republican party, to fill these offices for four years more, and I suppose that whatever controversy or contest you may have in other States, with the assistance of our colored friends in South Carolina you may be well assured that that State will give a cordial and overwhelming vote for the nominees of this Convention. [Great applause.]

I have felt more than ordinary solicitude, which has induced me to attend this convention, growing out of the many assaults which I have seen made on the President of the United States. If there was a contest here, it would, perhaps, be inappropriate to discuss the merits of any of the men who are to be presented; but the evidences are unmistakable here that the voice of the Convention, simply registering the instructions which we have received respectively from our constituents, will be the unanimous nomination of President Grant for re-election. [Applause.] I know that he has been arraigned; he has been maligned; he has been traduced. Has he been traduced or maligned more than General Washington? Was there ever a man who has filled the Presidential chair in the history of this Government who was subject to more assaults than Washington? He survived them, and the people that he carried through the bloody scenes of the Revolution re-elected him for four years, and when he had served eight years, he retired voluntarily.

The next great military hero that this country produced was General Jackson. At the end or before the expiration of his four years he was maligned all over the land and traduced, and yet the memory of the services which he had rendered to his countrymen in the war of 1812 carried him triumphantly a second time into the Presidential chair. Are the American people now, with the full recollection of the services rendered by General Grant in behalf of the Union, when they are enjoying the full fruition of those services, prepared to reverse the rule which was adopted with reference to those two illustrious heroes, his predecessors, and cast him aside? I don't believe it. [Great applause, and cries of "No, no, no! they won't."]

It is said that he has failed, failed morally, failed financially, failed in every respect as a President. Well, it may be that he has failed. That he has his faults, I have no doubt; but General Grant is not the man to fail. [Cheers.] When did he fail?

Where did he fail? On what field did he fail? I was upon the other side, and one of the great reasons why I think that my countrymen, in my own section of the United States, those who in former times, before the war, were associated with me in political life, should sustain him, is this, (and I have borne this testimony of him upon all occasions, from the beginning of the war to the end,) that while he made a gallant and finally a successful soldier, in all his intercourse with the armies of the rebel States he never once forgot the duties of the soldier or of the gentleman. [Wild applause.]

I believe myself that his re-election is a necessity to preserve peace in the country and peace abroad, and if he has failed I like such failures as he has given us within the last four years. [Renewed applause.] There is no sea that our flag does not float triumphantly upon. There is not a Court upon the face of the earth where the Government of the United States is not respected more than it has ever been before.

Your public debt is being extinguished, your public expenses are being reduced, and your taxation is being diminished. What more could a government do to make the people contented and happy, and induce them to give to those who are carrying it on their support and their votes? [Great applause.]

I come, gentlemen of the Convention, from the Ku-Klux region, and I desired and intended to have availed myself of the occasion some time, whilst in Philadelphia, to present to you some statistics which would perhaps enlighten you in respect to the outcry which has been raised by the Democratic party in the Southern States, and in the North and West also, about the outrages that have been committed. In South Carolina, as you are aware, in nine counties the writ of *habeas corpus* has been suspended—in a little over one-fourth of the entire State. The suspension embraced those counties where it was insisted that the State government was unable—it is unnecessary for me to discuss why—to give protection to men whose only offence was their political opinions and sentiments. They were colored men and white men, and when they went to sleep at night they had no guarantee that they would not be taken out of their beds at the dead hour of night; taken out and scourged, or else balls put through their bodies. This action on the part of President Grant was not taken until the Legislature of South Carolina passed resolutions and sent messengers to him calling upon him to send the forces of the United States Government there to give them protection. With reference to this Ku-Klux law President Grant had to execute the law. It was in the statute-book, and he was called upon to execute it by that tribunal which had the right to call upon him.

He performed the duty, and I have no doubt performed it cheerfully. He did not pass the law. How came it to be passed? Was it not the thunders of *The New York Tribune*, day after day and week after week, rung into the ears of Congress, demanding that they should pass some such law to give protection to these people? And now when the law is passed and has been executed in mercy and firmness, how stands my old friend Greeley? He has turned round now and denounces Grant and the Ku-Klux law for its enormities. Judge Bond has discharged his duties with great fidelity in South Carolina, has administered this law firmly and mercifully, and although you hear so much clamor, of people being cast into prison and not being able to procure bail, what is the result of the trials that have taken place? There have been about seven trials only at the two courts; one an acquittal, one a mistrial, and five convictions. Those are the results; and yet to show the extent of it, and how conclusive the proof was, not made up of manufactured testimony, or of testimony of suborned witnesses: more than sixty of these unfortunate people who have been indicted have voluntarily come forward and pleaded guilty to the charge preferred against them. Now when the facts come to be understood, I should suppose that, so far from being an element of weakness against the President, they would be an element of strength, because they prove beyond all controversy that when President Grant finds a law upon the statute-book he intends to execute it honestly and faithfully.

Gentlemen of the Convention, I thank you for the attention you have given me. I shall not detain you any further on this occasion. I trust that the proceedings of this body will be harmonious. I have no doubt that they will, but I hope that when we adjourn, and go forth to our respective homes, we will leave this place determined to fight a good fight and win the battle. In less than thirty days ten thousand voices will be raised, on every hill and in every valley upon the broad expanse of this great country, in favor of the nominees of this Convention, and in November, when the votes are counted, I have no doubt whatever that General Grant and his associate will be re-elected, and that the Republican party and principles will be established for the next four years. God grant it may be so. [Applause.]

General SHELBY M. CULLOM, of Illinois, in behalf of the Illinois delegation, asked that Governor RICHARD J. OGLESBY, of Illinois, be invited to address the Convention. [Loud cries of "Oglesby!" "Oglesby!"]

Governor OGLESBY appeared upon the platform and addressed the Convention as follows:

SPEECH OF GOVERNOR OGLESBY.

Mr. President and Gentlemen of the Convention: I have been listening for nearly two hours to some of the best speeches that have been made for a long time. You have first been entertained by the excellent and forcible speech of the temporary president of the Convention. After that you listened to the solemn words of invocation—one of the noblest and most fervent prayers that has ever been uttered in this city or this nation. You listened then to the Senator from Illinois, (General Logan,) who spoke for a few moments, and again to the Senator from Indiana, (Governor Morton,) who spoke at some length; but greatest and best of all, especially to those of us who never before have listened to his great words, we heard from that venerable, sublime man, of New York, who stood before us the impersonation of American dignity and American benevolence. [Great applause.]

I thought as the golden words fell from that oracle, that grand old agitator, how happy he must now be to realize the results of his long years of labor, when you and I were young and useless, as he saw before him here these colored men, redeemed and elevated to the high plateau of American freemen. [Renewed applause.]

The honorable Gerritt Smith has not only been a great instrument in the hands of God, before these American people, in lifting up this down-trodden and abused race, but he has taught you and me a little sense—to know and respect their rights. [Cheers.]

Why, this Republican party, as Senator Morton has said, is nothing more nor less than this great Republic. Without the Republican party the Republic would be nothing. [Cheers and cries of assent.] It has elevated us in the eyes of the world, in my opinion, to that high mark in American politics that no other party preceding it has, in our political history, ever attained before. In this convention to-day—neither a constitutional nor unconstitutional, but rather extra-constitutional body—the representatives of the outspoken sentiments of the respective States, speaking here for the whole people, that mighty tribunal before which politicians quake and tremble, have to record the solemn verdict of the Republican party of the United States. [Tremendous applause.] It is a solemn, grand result.

That little man, who but a few years ago was as unknown to fame and to this country as that poor colored man now redeemed and sitting in your midst; the young man who passed through West Point unnoticed, who passed through the Mexican war in the same way, unnoticed retired to private life. You and I know that among all the great names but a few years ago, this little man's name, Ulysses S. Grant, was unknown. I felt deeply grieved the other day by that great Senator from one of our grand States—that noble State that shines like a diamond on the Atlantic coast—that noble State which rocked the cradle of American liberty—that noble State that has ever stood first in behalf of human liberty—I felt really aggrieved in my own soul when I heard the voice, the grand, potent voice of the Senator from Massachusetts speak in such disrespectful language regarding the President, pronouncing against that man violent and disrespectful epithets, culminating with the weak, almost imbecile, charge that he was a tanner. What has been the history of General Grant? He went a stranger to West Point. He bore the ensign of his country as a subaltern officer in the Mexican war. He retired from the army and went into the ranks of private life, and, as an American citizen ought to do, when the hour came for him to support his wife and children, he went to work like an honest man. [Applause.]

How came the American people to select him for their general? Can you tell? Can history tell? No; no man can tell, unless it is written upon the necessities of the times by the invisible finger of Almighty God. [Applause.] Who brought him from obscurity? It was a mere circumstance in his life that he lived in our proud State. He came trudging along from obscurity step by step. He marched to the front. When the dark clouds of war were rolling and reverberating around the angry horizon; when none of us, not even our other gallant generals, our other magnificent soldiers in the East and West, worthy of all praise, worthy of all gratitude, when none of us knew where to look or what to do, this little shadow of Ulysses S. Grant fell upon us [applause] to give relief; and although that mighty voice assailed him but yesterday in the Senate, to-day the feeble voice of an obscure man who fought under his orders and by his side must now defend and uphold him. [Immense applause.] You, soldiers of the Potomac; you, soldiers of the East; you, soldiers of the West, and of all the land, you remember how unostentatiously and kindly, how generously, how confidingly he associated with and commanded us all. He was an enigma from the hour of his birth to this moment; his character has not yet been fathomed by this American people. He is purer and greater and nobler than we have ever thought him to be. Am I not an American citizen? Are you not, gentlemen, here with considerable responsibility upon your shoulders, representing your people? Are not you, and are not all of us American citizens, and have we not the same deep and vital interest in the perpetuity and the continuance of our Government that any other living mortal men can possibly have? I stand before you to-day, for one, uttering in my feeble way the voice of the great Prairie State, the State that gave to the country the immortal Lincoln. I come here to-day from that State with something of responsibility upon my shoulders, to speak for her free people, to say that our confidence to-day is unshaken in the deep and pure patriotism of General Grant, as has been shown in his magnanimity, and in his bright and shining intellect. [Applause.] He is not a man of words. He cannot utter a speech to defend himself at any time; upon no occasion can we hope for that, and therefore those of us who are gifted with speech—I am not sure but that some of us have a little too much of that element [laughter]—are quite free in our comments and strictures. Upon general grounds, and speaking for myself as one man, I claim as much interest in good government for myself and my children as any one can have in perpetuating this great Republic. But I come here to say, for myself, for you, and for the people whom we represent, that we have to-day perfect confidence in General Grant, and are willing to trust him four years longer, without so much as a shadow or suspicion of a doubt. [Applause.]

Those gentlemen who profess to believe the liberties of the people are in danger from the election of this man or that as President, are altogether mistaken in their estimate of the popular intelligence and popular patriotism if they suspect that General Grant, or any other living man, can destroy or tamper with the liberties of this great people. We tolerate incompetent officers; we tolerate unpalatable acts, but we suffer no man, great or small, to trifle with our liberties. The American people know how to defend themselves; they know how to protect their liberties. They are not alarmed at the cry of centralization of government, or of attempts on the part of this man or that to usurp power. We are greater than we used to be. We can afford to overlook many things that twenty-five years ago were sufficient to raise the cry that the rights of the States or the rights of the people were in danger. Some of these venerable relics of the past are still tramping round in our State, with the same cry. [Laughter.] Some of these men have been greatly honored and respected in the Republican party, and they regard it as their mission to instruct our people how to vote. Let me say to you gentlemen, gathered here in this Convention from all the States of this Union, to let Illinois alone. She will take care of herself. [Applause.] We know how to vote; we know how to discuss politics, and we know how to dispose of prominent gentlemen who have had no more prudence than to stumble and fall out of our gallant ranks as we are marching on. [Renewed applause.] There is no trouble in the State of Illinois, gentlemen, and I hope it will be so in every State in the Union. The public safety and the public security requires that this country shall still remain in the hands of its true and tried friends. No man doubts the fidelity of the Republican party to the principles of civil liberty. The people have confidence in us as the party of freedom and constitutional government. We do not hold the constitution of a State as the Brahmin holds his idol; we do not hold the constitution of any State as too sacred to be questioned when it is used for purposes of oppression and wrong. Oh, no, gentlemen, we bow to the majesty of the law; we abide by the requirements of our own State constitutions; we reverence the Constitution of the United States; but beyond constitutions, above constitutions, below constitutions, all around constitutions, stands this great American people, filled with common sense, deep, profound, unfathomable, and that American people will make and unmake constitutions. [Tremendous and long-continued applause.]

At the conclusion of the address there were loud calls for Governor JOSEPH R. HAWLEY, of Connecticut, who went upon the platform and said:

Mr. Chairman and Gentlemen of the Convention: I assure you that while I am gratified by this call, I am very greatly embarrassed also, for I desire to call for the report of the Committee on Permanent Organization. There may be other opportunities during the session of this Convention when I may desire to say a few words. It is not the time now for cool and deliberate argument. Will you, then, permit me now to call for the report of the Committee on Permanent Organization?

The Chairman stated he had just been informed that the committee is not ready to report.

Mr. M. D. BORUCK, of California. *Mr. President:* The delegates of California have heard with delight the distinguished speakers who have addressed us so eloquently in favor of the colored race and those delegates who represent them here in this Convention. California would like to hear a representative of that race speak for himself. [Great applause.]

There were continued calls for Grey, (colored delegate from Arkansas,) who was greeted with cheers upon taking the stand. He said:

SPEECH OF MR. WILLIAM H. GREY, OF ARKANSAS.

Gentlemen of the Convention: For the first time, perhaps, in the history of the American people, there stands before you in a National Convention assembled, a representative of that oppressed race that has lived among you for two hundred and fifty years, lifted by the magnanimity of this great nation, by the power of God and the laws of war, from the degradation of slavery to the proud position of American citizenship. [Great applause.] Words fail me, upon this occasion, to thank you for this evidence of the grandest progress in civilization, when a people of such magnitude, the grandest and greatest nation upon the face of the earth, not only in the recognition of the merits and of the glory of the war which her noble sons waged so successfully, have, in convention assembled, been willing to listen not only to the greatest of her orators, but to the humblest citizens of this great Republic. [Applause.]

I scarcely know where to begin upon an occasion like the present. If I raise the curtain of the past, then I open the doors of the sarcophagus from which we have but just emerged. If I should go back to the primary history of my race in this country, I would open up, perhaps, to discussion things and circumstances that would make us blush, and the blood in our cheeks to tingle in view of the evidences of the shameful and horrible condition—such in its degradation as the American people have never thought of—from which we have just escaped.

But this is scarcely necessary. We are ready to say in the words of the Good Book, "let the dead past bury its dead." While we remember these errors, while we remember all these degradations, there is no vengeance, thank God, found in our hearts. No revengeful feelings, no desire of retaliation. But God has given us a heart to thank the American people for the position in which we stand to-day, and we are willing, as I said before, to "let the dead past bury its dead," and to go on in our progress and fit ourselves to become what we have been made by law, American citizens in deed and in fact. [Applause.] It is the wonder of the world, the miracle of the nineteenth century, that in this tremendous struggle which rocked this great country from centre to circumference, that amid the debris of two hundred and fifty years, a living people were found by this great nation and lifted from degradation, as it were, by the strong arm of power, and at once, without preparation and without forethought, placed upon the broad plane of American citizenship. If we have failed somewhat in the sanguine expectation of our friends, yet, upon the whole, I think we have fairly worked out the problem so far as we have gone.

To-day, for the first time, God has pleased me with the sight of that grand, noble old man, Gerritt Smith, [applause,] who stood by us and for us when we could not stand for ourselves. [Tremendous applause.] The sight of him repays me for all the toil, all the suffering, all the pain of years. The sight of him renews' my faith in that humanity which is divine. [Cheers.] We are here to-day, gentlemen, a part and parcel of this great people, an integral part of the great body of this country, and here for the purpose, in harmony with you, of entrusting the reins of power into the hands of that hero who led us through a great and bloody struggle of years into the bright sunshine of liberty; led us out to citizenship, and who, when the war ended and he was nominated for President, in 1868, said, "Let us have peace." The solving of the problem of our citizenship has been the work of years. No one knew how that position was to be brought about. But few men could comprehend the situation or the political position of affairs in the South. Few men knew.

I happened to be present on that occasion, in Chicago, in 1868, when General Grant was nominated, and I know very well, and there are men here who can attest it, that through that political contest it cost the lives of over three hundred black men in Arkansas to carry the State for Ulysses S. Grant. To-day the problem is being worked out to further solution. The Ku-Klux problem is being worked out. The Ku-Klux situation is settled, and the peace of the country secured. But, had it not been for the passage of the Ku-Klux law and the man at the helm who had the nerve to execute it, that organization would be to-day in full venom in that section of the country. Therefore we urge upon the American people to give us Ulysses S. Grant for our candidate, for his name is a tower of strength at the South, and the only name that unrepentant rebels respect. [Prolonged cheers.] He is the man who is to work out the great problem now being solved in this country by the great Republican party;—as has been truly said, that problem has not yet been solved;—its duties are not entirely fulfilled; its organization must not yet be disintegrated. The full measure of our citizenship is not yet complete. We stand, many of us, in a prominent position in the Southern States; but right among the people where we hold these positions the law is so weak and the public sentiment so perverse that the common civilities of a citizen are withheld from us. We want the Civil Rights bill. [Applause.] We ask of the American people as the natural result of their own action that we shall be respected as men among men, and as free American citizens. [Cheers.] We do not ask that for any small reason. There are always two classes of people we have to be afraid of: that class who love us too well and that class who hate us too bad. [Laughter.]

All we ask is a fair chance in the race of life. Give us the same privileges and opportunities that are given to other men. I hope the action of this Convention will be such that we may be able to go home rejoicing. So far as the colored people of the South are concerned, they are a unit to-day for Ulysses S. Grant. [Cheers.] I know they told us after the Cincinnati Convention that "you niggers can now go for the father of Republicanism, Horace Greeley." When we objected to this on the ground that he was not the Republican nominee they said, "He is the father of Republicanism." Said I: "Very well; if that is so I thank him for having been the father of such a brood of illustrious and loyal men, but I fear, like Abraham of old, he takes Hagar instead of Sarah, and we cannot afford that." [Laughter.]

This is the inheritance of the free woman. This is the legitimate inheritance; these are the legitimate offspring, and we are going to keep the boys at home. [Laughter.] I am very much afraid that, like Hagar and Ishmael, the old lady will have to hunt water in the wilderness. [Great laughter.] The black people stand solid together. They know intuitively who is their friend; they know full well there is no standing for them outside the Republican party. They know they cannot afford to vote for men who say to them when they desire to vote, "You have got your rights now; what more do you want?" They cannot afford to vote for men who have refused to acknowledge or carry out the thirteenth, fourteenth, and fifteenth amendments to the Constitution. They cannot afford to vote against their own manhood, and they will not do it. Thank God, the colored men are Grant men with scarcely an exception to-day. [Applause.] God grant that the Republican party may close up its ranks and solidly march together, and victory will perch on its banners in the coming contest. [Prolonged cheering.]

Hon. R. B. ELLIOTT, M. C., a colored delegate from South Carolina, having been repeatedly called for from the audience, came to the stand and spoke as follows:

SPEECH OF MR. ELLIOTT.

Gentlemen of the Convention: It is with great appreciation of the compliment paid to my State that I rise to respond to your invitation to address this august assembly. I regret, however, that while accepting this invitation, I am compelled by the recognition of the fact that we are assembled here for the purpose of an important duty to the people of the nation, which duty is now pressing closely upon us, to ask you to excuse me from any extended remarks. I stand here, gentlemen of the Convention, together with my colleagues from the Southern States, to represent the people of my identity as an illustration of an accomplished fact in American emancipation. [Applause.] As an illustration, not only of the magnanimity of the American people, as stated by my distinguished friend from Arkansas, but also as a living example of the justice of the American Government, [applause,] we stand here in your midst, gentlemen, to assure you of the fact that we believe earnestly and faithfully in the principles of humanity and equal justice that you have asserted and maintained in the past. We stand forth to-day among you, not only to give our votes in this body in behalf of our constituencies for the nomination of President and Vice-President for the coming election, but also to pledge to you the earnest co-operation of the nine hundred thousand voters of our race, whose convictions are like unto your own. [Applause.]

We come here to-day to assure the delegates here assembled from the several States; we come here to assure the American people, that mindful of their services to us in the past, mindful of their goodness and of their justice, we intend to use the rights that have been given us, to use the privilege of the elective franchise, in the interest of the country, in the interest of the American people; and having a common interest with our fellow-citizens of whatever shade of complexion or from whatever part of the country, asking only what is just and fair, performing what is right, we mean to contribute our fair share and our full quota toward making our country what we conceive, along with you, it ought to be; a country that guarantees to all its citizens the equal protection of the law. [Applause.]

We will unite with you in making the American people the grandest and most powerful and purest in all respects of all the nations upon the face of the earth. We propose to unite with you, not only in protecting our citizens abroad, not only in having our banner waving all over this broad land, but that you may guarantee to all your citizens, whether they be among the lofty or the lowly, the equal protection of the laws at home.

Gentlemen, I will not attempt to detain the Convention from the purpose of its duties by any further remarks, but will simply say that the nine hundred thousand colored voters of America will stand by you in bringing success to the Republican party in the coming canvass upon the platform of justice and civil as well as political equality to all the people of the United States. [Applause.] Upon such a platform will we stand with you; we will pour out the gratitude of our hearts in most earnest devotion to our American institutions, and pour out upon them the rich oblation of earnest devotion. [Applause.]

Mr. HARRIS, a colored delegate from North Carolina, responding to repeated calls, spoke as follows:

SPEECH OF JAMES H. HARRIS.

It is not my purpose to detain this Convention. I cannot be oblivious of the fact that you have been in session already four long hours, and you must have become impatient in waiting for the report of the committee which we are now expecting. I do not appear upon this platform for the purpose of making a speech. I merely come forward to acknowledge the compliment paid, not to me, but to the loyal Republicans of North Carolina. [Applause.] I believe, sir, that no section of the country has gone through a more severe ordeal than the State of North Carolina. Ku-

Kluxers themselves can testify to that fact; and while I state that, I can also say that I believe, Ku-Kluxers permitting—and I suppose General Grant has convinced them that they must permit it—on the first day of August no State, North, South, East, or West, will give a better account of itself than the Republicans of North Carolina will do. I cannot trespass upon your time by asking you to listen to my speaking. [Cries of "Go on!"]

I assure you I am not one of those who have entertained the idea for a moment that this party—I mean the originators of the party—have ever grown weak-kneed—decided to abandon a single principle of our original platform—although they may not have carried out the civil rights bills in the way some of us desired. I have not agreed even with some of the colored Republicans who think we ought to be very careful about committing ourselves to the principles that shall be enunciated here. I have always believed that the political salvation of the negro and of the honest, hard-working people of the South rests with the Republican party. I believe, also, that this Convention will adopt a platform broad enough for every loyal man to stand upon; that it will, before adjourning, incorporate into the platform every vital principle contained in Sumner's civil rights bill. Then, when we go into the campaign, we can unfold our banner in the bright sun and pleasant breeze with the name of Ulysses S. Grant in letters of living light upon it. We will make a clean sweep, and Mr. Greeley and Liberalism will be known no more in this country. [Applause.]

I will say, in conclusion, that our Northern friends need not give themselves any fear that we are charmed with the name of Mr. Greeley, or that we have one eye toward Cincinnati. Although ignorant in the South, although we have not had the advantages of education, yet we know by instinct which side our bread is buttered on. [Laughter and applause.] But, although we may not comprehend the great political questions, let me tell you one thing, that the name of no man, or set of men, in this land will ever blind us so much as to make us forget the party that gave us liberty; that party which defends us, and which will lead us to a glorious future. [Applause.]

The CHAIRMAN. The Committee on Permanent Organization is ready to report.

REPORT OF COMMITTEE ON PERMANENT ORGANIZATION.

General ALBRIGHT, of Pennsylvania, the chairman of the committee, then reported the following as the

PERMANENT OFFICERS OF THE CONVENTION.

THOMAS SETTLE, of North Carolina, for President.

VICE-PRESIDENTS.

Alabama......................Paul Strobach.
Arkansas....................Elisha Baxter.
California....................H. S. Sargent.
Connecticut..................Sabin L. Sage.
Delaware.....................Isaac Jump.
Georgia.......................B. F. Conly.
Illinois......................Emery A. Storrs.
Indiana....................Sol. D. Meredith.
Iowa........................W. H. Seevers.
Kansas.................. John C. Carpenter.
Kentucky....................R. M. Kelley.
Louisiana...................Louis Frager.
Maine........................P. F. Robey.
Maryland....................Thomas Kelso.
Massachusetts..........Alexander H. Rice.
Michigan......................Eben B. Waul.
Minnesota...................C. T. Benedict.
Mississippi.................R. W. Flurnoy.
Missouri...................John F. Benjamin.
Nebraska...................John S. Bowen.

New Hampshire.......Wm. H. Y. Hackett.
New Jersey............Dudley S. Gregory.
New York....................H. B. Claflin.
North Carolina..........Edward Cantwell.
Ohio.........................Jacob Mueller.
Oregon.......................John P. Booth.
Pennsylvania................H. W. Olive.
Rhode Island..............A. E. Burnside.
South Carolina..............A. J. Ransier.
Tennessee ....William H. Wisner.
Texas......................A. B. Norton.
Vermont.....................J. Fairbanks.
Virginia.................Charles T. Malord.
West Virginia............Charles Horton.
Wisconsin................Lucien Fairchild.
Florida......................Dennis Eagan.
Colorado..............George M. Chilcott.
District of Columbia.......John F. Cook.
Idaho......................John R. McBride.
Wyoming..............John W. Donnellan.

SECRETARIES.

Alabama..................William V. Turner.	Nevada.......................C. C. Stevenson.
Arkansas.......................L. G. Wheeler.	New Hampshire...Charles S. Whitehouse.
California................Marcus D. Boruck.	New Jersey..................John W. Newlin.
Connecticut...............Daniel Chadwick.	New York..............D. Ogden Bradley.
Delaware........................Henry F. Pickles.	North Carolina..................T. A. Sykes.
Florida..........................J. W. Butler.	Ohio..........................James A. Sands.
Georgia.........................P. M. Shirtley.	Oregon.............................H. R. Kincade.
Illinois........................Daniel Shepard.	Pennsylvania................H. H. Bingham.
Indiana............................O. M. Wilson.	Rhode Island...........Wilson W. Aldrich.
Iowa..............................A. J. Felt.	South Carolina..............H. G. Maxwell.
Kansas..................Henry Buckingham.	Tennessee..................Thomas Waters.
Kentucky.........................T. C. Buerles.	Texas...............................G. T. Rubey.
Louisiana.........................E. L. Weber.	Vermont.........................W. Harris, Jr.
Maine...............................E. C. Brett.	Virginia........................John W. Woltz.
Maryland..........................W. G. Tuck.	West Virginia......................I. T. Hoke.
Massachusetts.........Charles E. Whiting.	Wisconsin.......................L. F. Frisby.
Michigan.......................C. S. Draper.	Colorado.................Jerome B. Chaffee.
Minnesota....................Otto Wallmark.	District of Columbia..Alex. R. Shepherd.
Mississippi.....................B. K. Bruce.	Idaho.................................E. J. Curtis.
Missouri..................Theodore Breuer.	Wyoming.................George W. Corey.
Nebraska........................J. B. Weston.	

The report of the committee was unanimously adopted.

General ALBRIGHT, of Pennsylvania. *Mr. Chairman:* The Committee on Organization desire to present the name of General H. H. Bingham, of this city, for the permanent Secretary of this Convention. He is the man to whom we are indebted for this fine building and the fine adornments we have here, and to the great welcome the delegates have received in the city of Philadelphia. I move he be made that Secretary.

The motion was adopted.

The CHAIRMAN. I have the honor to announce to the Convention that Judge Settle has just been unanimously elected President of this body, and will now take his seat.

The Hon. THOMAS SETTLE, of North Carolina, President elect, was then escorted to the chair, now vacated by Mr. McMICHAEL, and was received with enthusiastic and prolonged cheering, the audience rising to their feet. He addressed the Convention as follows :

ADDRESS OF THE PRESIDENT.

Gentlemen of the Convention: I thank you for the distinction of presiding over the deliberations of the greatest party in the greatest Power on earth; and I accept it, not so much as a personal tribute to myself, as the right hand of fellowship extended from our magnanimous sisters of the North to the erring, wayward, punished, regenerated, patriotic sisters of the South. [Immense applause.]

We have high duties to perform. We have assembled to name the man who shall administer the laws of the great Republic for the next four years; but our duties are plain. We shall be recreant to every trust and fail to respond to the vibrations of every patriotic heart if we do not, with one voice, name the soldier and patriot, Ulysses S. Grant, for the next President. [Renewed applause.]

We of the South recognize and demand him as a necessity for law and order in that portion of the country, and for the freedom of all men. [Applause.] It is not proper that I should detain you with extended remarks this evening. I shall, therefore, assume the duties which you have imposed upon me, and shall be very glad if an opportunity is afforded me to address you at greater length later in the session and when our labors shall have closed.

Mr. CHARLES S. SPENCER, of New York. *Mr. President:* I move that we adjourn until to-morrow at ten o'clock. A great many men are tired out, and we all wish rest now, that we may come fresh to the labors of that important day.

The motion was carried.

The PRESIDENT. The motion to adjourn is agreed to, and the Convention stands adjourned until to-morrow morning at 10 o'clock.

SECOND DAY—THURSDAY, JUNE 6, 1872.

At twenty minutes after ten o'clock the President of the Convention, Judge SETTLE, called the Convention to order.

Prayer was offered by Rev. Dr. HARPER, of the North Broad street Church, Philadelphia, as follows:

PRAYER.

Our Heavenly Father, Thou who rulest in Heaven, we invoke Thy presence and Thy blessing. We desire to begin this day that is to be memorable in the future and solve the destiny of this nation—we desire to begin, O Lord, this day with Thee. We come before Thee with a deep reverence for Thee. Preside over this assembly. Give them one mind and one heart. Help them to adopt the best measures. May the platform be the embodiment of the most humane principles. May the men selected be good and true men; may the land approve all they do. O Lord, we thank Thee for Thy care of us in days of adversity; let us not forget the ocean of blood through which we have passed. Bless the people, our rulers, the enfranchised, the immortal dead, the widows and children, and make us a blessing among the nations of the earth, and we shall ascribe all the praise to the Father, Son, and Holy Spirit, evermore. Amen.

ROLL-CALL.

Gen. H. H. Bingham, the permanent Secretary, then called the roll of States, and all were found present, with full delegations.

OREGON'S ELECTION.

Mr. DEVORE, of Oregon. *Mr. Chairman:* Oregon is redeemed. [Applause.] Oregon is redeemed both as to Representatives in Congress and her Legislature. [Renewed applause.] On last Monday an election was held in the State of Oregon. Four years we have been under Democratic rule. We are now Republican.

The Convention hailed the announcement with repeated outbursts of applause. A New Hampshire delegate proposed three cheers for Oregon, which were heartily given.

RULES AND ORDER OF BUSINESS.

The PRESIDENT announced as the business first in order the reception of the report of the Committee on Rules and Order of Business.

Mr. OLIVER AMES, of Massachusetts. *Mr. President:* The Committee on Rules and Order of Business respectfully report as follows:

Rule 1. Upon all subjects before the Convention, the States shall be called in alphabetical order, and next the Territories.

Rule 2. Each State shall be entitled to double the number of its Senators and Representatives in Congress according to the recent apportionment, and each Territory shall be entitled to two votes. The votes of each delegation shall be reported by its chairman.

Rule 3. The report of the Committee on Credentials shall be disposed of before the report of the Committee on Platform and Resolutions is acted upon, and the report of the Committee on Platform and Resolutions shall be disposed of before the Convention proceed to the nomination of candidates for President and Vice-President.

Rule 4. In making the nominations for President and Vice-President, in no case shall the calling of the roll be dispensed with. When it shall appear that any candidate has received the majority of the votes cast, the President of the Convention shall announce the question to be, "Shall the nomination of the candidate be made unanimous?" But if no candidate shall have received a majority of the votes the Chair shall direct the vote to be again taken, which shall be repeated until some candidate shall have received a majority of the votes cast.

Rule 5. When a majority of the delegates from any two States shall demand that a vote be recorded, the same shall be taken by States, the Secretary calling the roll of States in the order heretofore stated.

Rule 6. In the record of the vote by States the vote of each State shall be announced by the chairman; and in case the votes of any State shall be divided, the chairman shall announce the number of votes cast for any candidate, or for or against any proposition.

Rule 7. When the previous question shall be demanded by a majority of the delegation of any State, and the demand seconded by two or more States, and the call sustained by the majority of the Convention, the question shall then be proceeded with, and disposed of according to the rules of the House of Representatives in similar cases.

Rule 8. No member shall speak more than once upon the same question, nor longer than five minutes, unless by leave of the Convention, except that delegates presenting the name of a candidate shall be allowed ten minutes to present the name of such candidate.

Rule 9. The rules of the House of Representatives shall be the rules of this Convention, so far as they are applicable and not inconsistent with the foregoing rules.

Rule 10. A Republican National Committee shall be appointed, to consist of one member from each State, Territory, and District represented in this Convention. The roll shall be called, and the delegation from each State, Territory, and District shall name, through their chairman, a person to act as a member of such committee.

OLIVER AMES, *Chairman.*

D. VICKERS, *Secretary.*

The report was unanimously agreed to.

REPORT OF THE COMMITTEE ON CREDENTIALS.

The President next called for the report of the Committee on Credentials.

Mr. ISAAC PENDLETON, of Iowa, chairman. *Mr. President:* The Committee on Credentials respectfully report that there are present full delegations from all the States and Territories, and that no seats are contested, except those of Utah and Dakota. The committee have decided to admit the four delegates from Dakota, giving them the right to two votes in the Convention. In the case of Utah the committee have decided that the delegation represented by A. S. Gould and O. J. Hollister is the more regular, and are therefore entitled to their seats.

[The report of the committee in detail is given in an appendix.]

A DELEGATE from California. *Mr. President:* I desire to move an amendment to the report, and I do not know whether this is the proper time to move that amendment. I have understood that there being a contest among the delegates from Utah, one set, and the regular set of delegates from that Territory, were ruled out because of their being Mormons. I therefore move that the report be amended so as to admit both sets of delegates, as was done in the other case. [Cries of "No!" "No!"]

The PRESIDENT. The question is upon the amendment.

Mr. E. B. STODDARD, of Massachusetts. The gentleman is mistaken in regard to the decision of the committee. It was made upon the ground that the delegates who were reported against were not elected at a duly called convention. This is the substance of the report of the committee. [Cries of "Question!"]

Mr. CHARLES S. SPENCER, of New York. These gentlemen, sir, have come a long way here from Utah. There are but two of them. I shall support the amendment; I think we had better marry them all. [Laughter and applause.]

Mr. GEORGE WURTS, of New Jersey. *Mr. President:* In the committee I moved precisely this compromise, but the delegates whose exclusion is recommended declined to accept it.

The amendment was lost, and the report of the committee as originally presented was adopted, with a single dissenting voice.

THE NATIONAL EXECUTIVE COMMITTEE.

The PRESIDENT. While waiting for the report of the Committee on Resolutions the Secretary will call the roll of States for nomination of members of the National Executive Committee.

The Secretary then called the roll, with the following result:

Alabama	George E. Spencer.
Arkansas	Powell Clayton.
California	George C. Gorham.
Connecticut	Marshall Jewell.
Delaware	George Riddle.
Florida	William H. Gleason.
Georgia	Isham S. Fanning.
Illinois	J. Y. Scammon.
Indiana	O. P. Morton.
Iowa	Grenville W. Dodge.
Kansas	John A. Martin.
Kentucky	William C. Goodloe.
Louisiana	G. Casanave.
Maine	William P. Frye.
Maryland	C. C. Fulton.
Massachusetts	William Claflin.
Michigan	William A. Howard.
Minnesota	John T. Averill.
Mississippi	O. C. French.
Missouri	R. T. Van Horn.
Nebraska	E. E. Cunningham.
Nevada	James W. Nye.
New Hampshire	William E. Chandler.
New Jersey	Alexander G. Cattell.
New York	Edwin D. Morgan.
North Carolina	Joseph C. Abbott.
Ohio	B. R. Cowen.
Oregon	Joseph G. Wilson.
Pennsylvania	William H. Kemble.
Rhode Island	William D. Brayton.
South Carolina	Franklin J. Moses, Jr.
Tennessee	Horace Maynard.
Texas	E. J. Davis.
Vermont	George Nichols.
Virginia	H. H. Wells, Jr.
West Virginia	Hanson Criswell.
Wisconsin	David Atwood.
Arizona	John Titus.
Colorado	Edward M. McCook.
Dakota	William H. H. Beadle.
District of Columbia	Henry D. Cooke.
Idaho	John R. McBride.
Montana	Lucius B. Church.
New Mexico	Joseph G. Palen.
Utah	Alfred S. Gould.
Washington	L. B. Andrews.
Wyoming	William T. Jones.

As the names were announced nearly all were received with hearty applause.

The nominations were unanimously confirmed.

RESOLUTIONS REFERRED.

Ex-Governor PARSONS, of Alabama. I offer the following resolutions, which I desire read:

Resolved, That we earnestly desire peace with all nations as the greatest earthly blessing, and the continuation of friendly relations with them, founded on principles of justice and right. To accomplish these great ends we are willing to make all proper concessions. The spirit has characterized our intercourse with the people and government of Great Britain.

Resolved, That in view of existing circumstances, we deem it proper to declare that, in our judgment, when these means fail, our "English cousins" will find the people of the United States of this day as firmly resolved and united in the maintenance of our rights and honor as our fathers were in 1776 and 1812; and that we will uphold the hands of our Government in asserting them, without distinction of party or section, as our fathers have taught us, "with our lives, our fortunes, and our sacred honor."

Resolved, That the "Trent affair" was settled at the time by the prompt action of our Government before the act complained of was made known by the British government, and that we commend this example to favorable consideration with respect to the "Alabama claims," which must also be settled, by peaceable means or otherwise.

Mr. STEVENS, of New Jersey. *Mr. President:* In order to save time and facilitate business, I desire to move that the remainder of the resolutions and all others be referred, without debate and without reading, to the committee on Resolutions.

A Delegate from Maryland moved that the resolutions lay on the table. Lost.

The motion of Mr. Stevens was adopted.

Mr. ROBINSON, of Louisiana. I have a resolution I desire to offer, and I ask that it be read without referring to the Committee on Resolutions.

The PRESIDENT. Under the order just adopted the resolution cannot be read.

Mr. Jones, of Alabama, offered a resolution, which was referred without reading or debate.

RESOLUTIONS OF THE UNION LEAGUE OF AMERICA.

Mr. McMICHAEL, of Pennsylvania. I desire to present a communication from the Union League of America, and ask that it be read.

The Convention, on motion, granted leave, and the communication and accompanying resolutions were read, as follows:

PHILADELPHIA, *June 5*, 1872.

To the President and Members
of the National Republican Convention:

Agreeably to the action of the National Council of the Union League of America, at its meeting in this city on the 4th instant, we have the honor to present to you the accompanying paper, expressive of the views and principles of the organization which we represent.

Respectfully,

JOHN W. GEARY, *President.*

T. G. BAKER, *Secretary.*

JAMES BUCHANAN, New Jersey,
W. J. P. WHITE, Pennsylvania,
T. L. CARDOZA, South Carolina,
WILLIAM A. COOK, District of Columbia,
C. C. PINCKNEY, New York,
J. H. HARRIS, North Carolina,
J. H. JOHNSON, Arkansas,

Committee.

The members of THE UNION LEAGUE OF AMERICA, IN NATIONAL COUNCIL assembled, do hereby affirm their adherence to the following sentiments and principles:

First. We reject, as utterly unfounded, the idea that the mission of the Republican party has been accomplished, and that no necessity exists for its continuance. By its principles and actions the nation was saved during the period of the late rebellion, and by them must it be preserved and exalted in coming time.

Second. Whatever may be its pretences, the Democratic party remains unchanged in character and ultimate purposes. What it was from April, 1861, to April, 1865, it still is, and will continue to be. Incapable of reform or improvement, it will always be unfit to direct or govern the nation.

Third. In the so-called Liberal Republican party we find no attractive political virtue and no important distinctive principle. It is manifestly an organization created by personal designs, and by feelings so embittered and intense that it is prepared and solicitous to form an alliance with the Democratic party, as the only possible method of accomplishing its narrow and unjustifiable purposes. This fact alone develops its true nature; and it requires no other to present it to the people, as inherently base and ignoble, and altogether undeserving of their approval and support.

Fourth. All American citizens, without distinction of race, color, or religion, are entitled to the same civil and political rights, and to equal and exact justice before the laws, subject only to the Constitution of the United States.

Fifth. The system of terrorism which so long infested, and still exists, in some portions of the South, must be put down at all hazards, and the guilty parties punished as other outlaws and murderers are punished.

Sixth. We earnestly urge the House of Representatives to pass the civil rights and enforcement bills pending before it; and it is our profound conviction that Congress should not adjourn until these bills shall become laws.

Seventh. The wisdom of the adoption of the thirteenth, fourteenth, and fifteenth amendments to the Constitution has been fully demonstrated by their practical operation, and we will earnestly oppose any attempt, open or insidious, to either repeal them or weaken their force.

Eighth. We believe the national debt, contracted to save the life of the nation, should be paid to the uttermost farthing, according to the letter and spirit of the laws which authorized it. This payment should be steady but gradual, so as to avert oppressive taxation, and distribute a portion of the burden upon the vastly increased wealth and population of future years.

Ninth. All tariff and internal taxation needed for the reduction of the public debt and for the support of the Government should be so adjusted as to bear with least weight upon the laboring classes, and to foster and encourage the industries of the nation, which are the foundation of all national prosperity.

Tenth. We favor the reform of the civil service so that capacity and integrity, and not political influence alone, shall be the tests for office; and we have no faith in the accomplishment of that reform by the party which originated the maxim, "To the victor belongs the spoils," and which has faithfully observed the maxim whenever there were any spoils to divide.

Eleventh. The administration of President Grant is one which is approved by the calm, sober sense of the nation, and however much it may be misrepresented by those whose hatred of the man dates back to the times of his victories over the rebels in the field, or by others whose narrow jealousies or ambitious aspirations have led them to array themselves against him, the fact that during his administration three hundred and thirty-two millions of the public debt have been paid; the premium on gold has become nearly nominal; the revenue taxes have been greatly reduced and faithfully collected; civil service reform has been successfully inaugurated; and an acquiescence, real or pretended, in all the cardinal principles the Republican party has urged during the past years, been obtained, has strengthened his hold upon the confidence of the people no less than his splendid victories in the field had endeared him to their hearts.

The reading of the resolutions was received with demonstrations of approval by the Convention.

Mr. GEORGE B. LORING, of Massachusetts. *Mr. President:* The organization presenting these resolutions is entitled to the respect of every Republican in the United States. It has done more than almost any existing association that I know of to keep the Republican sentiment strong before the people from the opening of the war to this hour. The President of that association, with whose name every loyal American is familiar, and who has done so much for the State over whose councils he presides, is also entitled to the affection and regard of every Republican of every State. The name of Governor Geary is dear to every Republican, North and South. Now, sir, it is on this account that I desire to step out of our usual channel and to move that these resolutions be entered on the records of this Convention and be printed with the proceedings.

The Chairman put the motion to the Convention, and it was unanimously adopted.

Mr. WEBSTER FLANAGAN, of Texas. *Mr. President:* Yesterday this Convention was edified by orators from various portions of the Union. We heard only from those who were loyal during the war. We heard those who were opposed to secession. Texas feels that she has a right to be heard, and asks that she be heard in the person of General George W. Carter, who was the leader of one of the Southern brigades in the late rebellion. I had the honor, and I am glad to express it, of being an humble private in that soldier's corps, and I ask that he be heard on this occasion.

Cries for " Carter !" " Carter !" " Speech !" &c., were heard.

Colonel GEORGE W. CARTER then proceeded upon the platform and spoke as follows:

REMARKS OF COLONEL GEORGE W. CARTER.

Mr. President and Gentlemen of the Convention: I appreciate your desire to hear something of the Republican candidates from a Confederate, who believed he was right, although a speech from me at this time may not be very appropriate. I am an ex-Confederate soldier who needed reconstruction, and if I am any judge in the matter, I believe that I have been reconstructed. I came out of the war with only two planks in my platform. One was from the Democratic platform, which was, if I could not get what I wanted, to take what I could get. The other was a philosophical plank, to have no prejudices, and that a whipped man was not entitled to his prejudices. I think I am a type of the men who fought honestly and got whipped squarely on that question. We have come through the war, and have learned lessons which we think will be valuable. I think our people down there are learning. One of the lessons we have learned is this, that the will of the American people is to be respected. [Applause.]

The Hollander was our type of the revolutionist. We have now taken the French type, that when we get whipped, if the country won't follow us we will follow it. We came out of the war with that purpose, and you will find it in the South to-day in the Presidential election approaching, and if the issue is made between Grant and Greeley, the Southern people who were honest in their convictions, and have abandoned their abstractions as far as they entered into the fight, prefer an honest, practical man, who makes them behave themselves. [Applause.] They prefer a man who does not cry over them as they weep over their distresses, but tells them they must work if they would be happy; that the true remedy for the evils under which they labor is to go to work and adjust themselves to the condition of the country as they find it in their new relations. I believe to-day if the Democrats endorse Mr. Greeley, General Grant will get more straight Democratic votes than Greeley will in Louisiana. [Applause.]

In response to loud calls, Mr. STROBACH, of Alabama, took the stand and said:

SPEECH OF MR. PAUL STROBACH.

Gentlemen of the Convention: It is with great diffidence that I approach the stand this morning. I understood that yesterday I was called for, as great desire was expressed to hear from a naturalized citizen, but I was absent at the moment. I did not expect to speak to-day, because I thought there was no necessity. You already know how the naturalized citizen in his gratitude feels for this adopted country of his. I saw this morning in one of the papers a slur on the Convention, alleging that it did not allow the naturalized citizen to be heard. In presence of all, allow me to return my sincere thanks to you for the honor conferred upon me in making me one of the Vice-Presidents of this Convention, which, in my opinion, represents the only true and unselfish patriots of this great country—the Republicans.

I will take the liberty of speaking to you first as a citizen of my adopted State, Alabama, and then as one of those who represent what is called the German element. We number twenty delegates from the Southern States, and I saw a newspaper this morning which called this Convention a convention of office-holders and office-seekers. None of the delegates from Alabama are office-holders under the Federal Government. None of us are office-seekers. We can have offices, if we want them, at home from the hands of our Republican friends. I had the honor to represent my county for four years in our legislature in that cradle of secession—Montgomery—and in the hall where William L. Yancey taught his pernicious doctrines. I was sent there by an overwhelming majority of Republicans, and at the last election they made me sheriff of my county. But I am no office-seeker. I am here, I trust, actuated by true, patriotic motives.

One of the distinguished orators said on yesterday that he came from the Ku-Klux region. I am not from that region, but I know something about it. Many outrageous and terrible crimes have been committed in my adjacent neighborhoods by bands of disguised, midnight assassins, and, wherever that hell-born organization exists, it will need the strong arm of the Government to protect Republicans. I will mention one instance: in the jail of my county are confined 33 United States prisoners, a majority of them having been committed under the Ku-Klux law. One of the most terrible crimes which has ever disgraced the pages of history will be tried to-day in Montgomery, before Judge Busteed. The case is one in which a colored man and his wife were burned alive, and the man's only crime was that he had married a white woman. I tell you that I consider that a matter of taste. It is nobody's business who a man marries. If that white woman desired to marry that colored man, no one else had anything to do with it. This band of assassins went at the hour of midnight, and destroyed their little cabin, and after killing the husband, *burned the wife alive.* This is one of the many instances to show you that the Ku-Klux are not as the Democratic papers represent them, a myth, for there are facts and accusations so plain that we must have the strong arm of the Government to protect us in the South. While if we should have the philosopher Greeley as our next ruler, I am confident that the Republicans of the South will suffer. I hope, therefore, that you will give us as our next ruler the man who is able and willing to make the people down there respect our rights for all time to come, *I mean Gen. Grant.* Among other arguments which I have heard sneeringly used against President Grant—not counting the abuse and calumny heaped upon him by the great Massachusetts Senator a few days since, which, by the way, gave Grant more sympathy and votes than Mr. Sumner dreamed of—is this: that he is not a great speaker. But we don't want a man of speech; we want a man of will and action. But yet I remember that Gen. Grant made three speeches, which are engraved with an iron pen in the book of history, and which will endear him forever to the Union-loving people of this country. The first was when he said, "I will fight it out on this line, if it takes all summer." The second was at Belmont, when he said, "We whipped them once, and I hope to God we will whip them again;" and the third and noblest speech of this great captain, who knew that every battle of the war had crowned his brow with laurels, was when he said, "LET US HAVE PEACE."

I ask if you do not find more force, more justice, and especially more patriotism, in those three little speeches, than in all the late oratorical displays of the renowned Senators from Massachusetts and Missouri?

And now, gentlemen, let me approach one subject, which I touch with almost bleeding heart, being compelled to arraign before you a countryman and friend of mine; a man who has worked faithfully for the Republican party in the past, but who seems to be parting with his old love for unaccountable or ambitious reasons. Out of the many indictments preferred by the Republicans against him, I will arraign him before you to-day on one only. Gentlemen, I love my fatherland and am not ashamed of it. I know that every native-born American will respect me the more for it. But beyond this love for my mother country—which gave me only birth—I cherish a deep and undying love, mingled with eternal gratitude, for my adopted country, which gave me a home and fireside for my wife and children, and I would rather allow my tongue to cleave to the roof of my mouth before uttering one word of abuse against my home and government, to bring my adopted country into disgrace and difficulty with a foreign power, even though it be my mother country. I tell you, gentlemen, that were I to live to be as old as Methuselah, I could never atone for this crime. And yet that man upon whom the people, and especially Republicans, have bestowed the highest position with which the American people can honor an adopted citizen, has committed that crime under a frivolous pretext; but thanks to the wisdom of our government, and the man who controls the diplomacy of the old fatherland, it resulted in nothing but a little oratorical display and waste of precious time.

But, gentlemen, I am confident that the Republican party, like an affectionate, forbearing, and forgiving mother, will be willing to take back the erring son into its fold, when he is willing to acknowledge that the false Democratic prophets deceived him and a few of his followers for the accomplishment of their own aims and the destruction of the Republican party. But if he should insist, in his incomprehensible blindness and self delusion, in continuing this unholy war for the only purpose of delivering the Republican party, hand and foot, to its arch ememy, he will be left alone, deserted by his former allies, and the great Senator from Missouri will not have a corporal's guard of his Republican countrymen to attend his political funeral. An overwhelming majority of the adopted German sons of this great and free country will turn to the old flag in peace, as they did in war, and march on, as in 1868, to the great Republican victory in 1872.

Calls were next made for "Storrs of Illinois!" and in response thereto Mr. EMERY A. STORRS came to the platform.

SPEECH OF E. A. STORRS.

Mr. Chairman and Gentleman of the Convention: This magnificent assemblage of people doesn't look very much as if the mission of the Republican party was ended. I represent in part the greatest carpet-bag State in the Union—the State of Illinois—for in our delegation there is but one man born in the State. [Applause.] We came to that State without even a carpet-bag.

We came there with nothing but lessons of earnest work and resolute purpose, and high heart and strong will, that we had learned in our old Eastern and New England homes. In twenty five years the carpet-baggers of Illinois have built a magnificent empire, and, on the shores of that great lake, one of the most magnificent cities that the world has ever seen. I say, then, that if the carpet-bag tree produces this kind of fruit, for God's sake plant it all over the nation. [Cheers.] As proud as I was of my great city a year or two ago, I was prouder still of it after the flames had swept over it, when, out of the still unextinguished fires, I saw the spirit of the carpet-bagger rising unconquered and unconquerable.

They claim that the mission of the Republican party is ended, and that its work is done. It has never made a promise it has not kept; it never made an engagement it has not performed; it never entered into any contract it has not executed, and therefore, I suppose, its mission has terminated! It is one of those parties stronger than its leaders. I remember one day we discharged a whole cabinet of leaders, and it operated like a tonic, and we were stronger for the exercise the next morning. The pathway of the Republican party is strewn with the carcasses of its leaders. The party goes after its leaders when those leaders go to the place where the rank and file desire to go. It is stronger than platforms, for the platforms of the Republican party are written upon the hearts of the rank and file in a language above that inscribed in the records of our conventions. [Cheers.] And the conventions take their law from the rank and file; they do not give it to the rank and file. We know to-day what the platform of the Republican party is, and what the platform of the Republican party will be. We are told, however, that our great chieftain has been untrue to the cause which he represents and unfaithful to the principles upon which he was elected, and Mr. Sumner, in a recent speech, made these charges. Let me say that the Republican party has always been a party of deeds and not of words—a party of achievements and not merely a party of promises; and that so far as history is concerned, the record of what our great captain has done, and the deeds he has accomplished, will live in the pages of history long after the speeches of Sumner and his other defamers shall have gone into oblivion.

I will not detain you longer, my fellow-citizens, than to say that the people of this country cannot forget and will not forget the great achievements which Ulysses S. Grant has accomplished in the redemption of this land, nor the great deeds which he has written on the records of the nation's history; and when the hour shall come they will give voice to their gratitude by a larger majority than any President ever yet received, in the election of Ulysses S. Grant as his own successor. [Great applause.]

A DELEGATE from California. I desire to inquire whether the Committee on Resolutions is ready to report. We understand the order of business requires the platform to be adopted, and we desire that to be done so that we can proceed to the nomination of Grant. [Applause.]

The PRESIDENT. I am informed that the committee will be ready to report in a half hour.

Hon. H. T. BLOW, of Missouri. *Mr. President:* The delegates of this State ask a favor of this Convention, if it is pleasant to grant it. We have in our midst a distinguished representative of Missouri, familiar with the politics of the nation, and especially of his own State of Missouri. We ask that you will listen to John B. Henderson.

In response to general calls from the audience, Hon. JOHN B. HENDERSON rose in his place in the Convention, and spoke as follows:

SPEECH OF EX-SENATOR HENDERSON.

Mr. President and Gentlemen of the Convention: You want to hear something of Missouri politics. Well, Missouri politics for the last two years have been a little misty. We have so many great men in Missouri that it is exceedingly difficult to satisfy them all. [Laughter.] I cannot, my fellow-citizens, when you are so restless and weary, attempt to address you, and I have said to our delegation not to insist upon it. It is not well to press remarks upon a body when they are not inclined to listen. We came here for the purpose of making nominations. After these are made, I will, with your good-will, select an opportunity of addressing a few words to this body. Wait till the resolutions are adopted, and I have a text to talk to you on. I might not talk in exactly the orthodox manner. I have my choice in regard to the selections to be made for the offices of President and Vice-President, but let me tell you, however, that after you shall have made the nominations, I, for one, shall give them my most hearty support; and whatever you may think of Missouri, I am here to say that now the Republican party of that State is united. [Applause.] There will come up from the prairies and from the valleys of that State one universal shout for the nominations of this Convention. [Applause.] It has been a most unfortunate quarrel in our State, but it is healed now. There have been Liberals and regulars, but now they are upon the same platform. [Applause.] Some of us in the State favored the repeal of constitutional restrictions against those who had been engaged in the rebellion. I, for one, after the war was over, and we had secured everything we could, was in favor of the constitutional amendments adopted by the Republican party to enfranchise the rebels; not that they deserved it, but simply because it was dangerous in a republican government to keep a part of her citizens excluded, and I therefore went for repealing the constitutional restrictions.

But, my fellow-citizens, the nominee in Missouri having received the support of the Democratic party (and it always seemed dangerous to receive it from that party,) after his re-election seemed to feel greater obligations to the Democracy of the day than to the Liberal portions of the Republican party. Unfortunately he left us, he went astray, and now we wish him all the success that he can possibly have except an election upon the tail of the Liberal Republican ticket. After that election was over, I, for one, supposed that all the elements of separation, and all that had kept us from harmoniously working together, had disappeared, and that there was no reason why the party should not unite. It is united, and we wish our friend Carl Schurz would be with us. But it seemed that this enfranchisement alone was not enough, and immediately after the election they brought on a new issue. They wanted free trade. Well, gentlemen, we are rather a free-trade State in Missouri. We should be for free trade, if we had no debt. But we do not believe in running this great Government for our exclusive benefit. We realize the amenities of life, we are a clever people, and understand the various wants of this great nation.

Although our State is largely a farming State, and would be largely benefited by a low tariff, our people are not so wild that they do not recognize the rights of others, and in levying a tariff for revenue they could not overlook the great interests of the great industries of Pennsylvania and other States of the nation. [Applause.] Our friend Schurz went to Cincinnati and secured an equivocal platform, and the father of high tariff is the candidate that stands upon it. I understand that in a short time he is to visit Europe, and, I suppose, for the purpose of getting a large supply of "pretzel seed" for his candidate. [Laughter and applause.]

Mr. W. D. BICKHAM, of Ohio. *Mr. President:* I move a suspension of the rules, and that we proceed to ballot for President of the United States.

The PRESIDENT. There is a rule just reported and adopted that until the platform is adopted no ballot for President shall take place. We are informed that it will be some time before the committee can report. It is moved and seconded that the rule which prohibits a ballot for a candidate for President be suspended, and the Convention proceed to nominate a President. As many as are in favor of that motion will say aye.

The motion was lost.

Mr. HILL, of Mississippi. *Mr. President:* I desire to suggest that while the various delegations are presenting to this Convention, from different sections, eloquent orators, we propose to this Convention that it listen to the eloquent colored Secretary of State from Mississippi, Hon. James R. Lynch.

Mr. LYNCH was loudly called for, and advancing to the platform, said:

ADDRESS OF JAMES R. LYNCH, OF MISSISSIPPI.

Mr. President: Standing in this grand presence, after the eloquent expression that was given to the feelings and opinions of the colored people of our country on yesterday, and appreciating the value of your time, I should be constrained to silence on this occasion, knowing that the 400,000 colored people of the State of Mississippi, and the Republicans of other color, are waiting with anxious hope to hear the announcement by telegraph that Gen. Grant has been renominated for President of the United States. [Great applause.]

I will not trespass on your valuable time by entering into any argument in favor of the Republican party. It needs no more argument to convince patriotism, justice, reason, and intelligence that it is the only party that can bless and save the country, and realize the hopes of its founders, than does the glorious sun, scattering his rays everywhere, bathing the world in glory, to make men believe that it is necessary to warm our air to make it capable of supporting human life. [Great applause.]

I heard gentlemen say here that we would kill the Democratic party. With all due deference to those who have superior political sagacity and knowledge to that which I possess, I beg leave to suggest that the Democratic party is dead. [Laughter.] Some may ask, then, why fulminate against it from the platform? why resolve against it? why invoke the Divine Master to retard its progress? Because a dead body lying on the ground in the summer time may do more harm than a living one. [Roars of laughter.] I behold this Democratic party dead; its hydra head in the waters of the Lakes, its great cloven feet stuck out in the waters of the Gulf, one of its cold, clammy, bony fingers grasps the Pacific and the other the Atlantic, and the stinking carcass emits an odor that breeds disease, and that disease threatens the Union soldier, one-armed and one-legged, and the widows and orphans, clothed in the habiliments of mourning, with national disgrace. That contagion threatens the nation with repudiation; threatens men who, in the field, in the Cabinet, and in the national councils, saved to the world the glorious heritage and the hope which made the victims of European despotism and tyranny smile amid their tears as in chains they were confined within the walls of the bastiles and dungeons all over Europe. It threatens them with disgrace, and we propose to turn out next November in the State of Mississippi, with the colored citizens all over our broad land, under the leadership of General Ulysses S. Grant, now President of the United States, and dig a grave for this corpse, so deep and so wide, and bury it so that it will never more be resuscitated. [Applause.]

Mr. President, I will not detain you. [Cries of "Go on!"] There are some reasons why the colored people of the United States cling to the Republican party. We look to the Republican party as our political parents. We are born of them. Have you any guarantee of the fidelity of colored men in the Republican party? You have the same guarantee that fathers all over the land, wherever civilization beams, have for the filial and faithful regard of their children. [Cheers.] We are, then, true to the Republican party; and while we love the people of the South, and while we ask for concord, for peace and harmony, while we recognize the fact of the identity of interest between white and black, that the ex-rebels of the South are identified and interwoven in all the interests of social life, of material wealth, and all that concerns it, yet we mean to walk in the pathway hewn out by the sword. Any concession we could make that would not sacrifice our political equality we would make.

But, Mr. President, we rejoice that the Republican party has made a sentiment, and gives expression to it in this great Union, that our Republic, like the rainbow, is not complete without its darkest color. [Laughter and applause.] We stand here asking no particular advantage, no special favor, but simply to be recognized as an equal in the body politic of this great land.

Opposition to General Grant means more than opposition to nepotism; more than opposition to the great soldier of Island No. 10 and the conqueror of the rebellion. It means opposition to the principles that triumphed during the war. [Applause.] Tell me not that because Mr. Greeley was the great apostle of liberty; tell me not because his gray hairs are associated with the noblest and grandest work for humanity, that the colored people will recognize any magic power in that name. Aye, sir, the name of Ulysses S. Grant was imprinted in their hearts and memories, revealed to them by the thunder of war, by the lightning flash of musketry, when their hearts were melted lava, burning with a desire for freedom. Then was Grant's name written.

Every regiment, every squad of United States forces that advanced upon the South under your Logans, under your Howards, under your Shermans and Gearys, that unfolded the star-spangled banner and dropped the boon of liberty at every cabin door, bound their hearts to President Grant by cords that cannot be separated. [Applause.] The colored people of the United States are gravitating toward the South. The semi-tropical and tropical portions of our great country—a vast untilled country and of undeveloped resources—our country, foremost in the family of nations, representing advanced intelligence, Christianity, and moral power, exceeding, in all these, any portion of the world—must soon make Mexico, the West Indies, and Central America part of ourselves, as is Alaska. [Cheers.] These new countries, with their wealth of centuries, with their mahogany wood, with their mines, their wonderful harbors, and their undeveloped resources, cannot be developed, cannot enrich the world, cannot subserve the purposes of American civilization without the black man's muscle. Without the black man the cotton States cannot be developed. They have tried to supplant the black man by the introduction of the Swedes, and Danes, and English, but it has been such a sad failure that the distinguished men who have attempted it are now ashamed to confess that they ever embarked in it. The Democrats in the political canvass of the South are now looking to the Southern black men and begging them for their votes. They cry out as did a certain warrior in the turbid waters of the Tiber, asking his companions to save him lest he sink. With their lands worn and barren, with their capital gone, with their houses dilapidated, with their industry gone, with their resources vanishing, they cry to the black man from a material stand-point, "Save us, or we sink!" [The applause was continued some time.] Is this an attempt to put down President Grant? [The applause was renewed.] The experience of the past has convinced me that applause admits of two interpretations, [laughter,] therefore I will have regard for time. No; if you do not nominate President Grant—which your Brick Pomeroys are invoking God you will not—if they have any God—you cannot do him any harm. His fame is immortal; great names and deeds go not down to silence, but history embalms their memory with undying honors, and minstrels catch up the glowing theme, and send it echoing all along the archways of time.

Mr. President, Grant will be a strong candidate at the South. The name of Greeley inspires no heartfelt enthusiasm. That man who had the genius to command your armies when the nation was incredulous of success; that man who could stand reverses; who, disregarding alike the bickerings and jealousy of petty rivalry, could move on with grandeur and unswerving will to the conquest of the rebellion, understands the wants of this great country. I believe his heart to-day goes forth to the South, and he would, if he could, lift the disabilities from every one of its citizens and declare universal amnesty. Ah! our Southern people have much to learn. I tell them this at home: I tell them this everywhere. Instead of basking in the light of this great candle of liberty which is destined to dispel their darkness; instead of putting their fingers into it and burning them, or else blowing it out for fun, and complaining because we will not let them do this, they must say, No, you must stand still; you must let this candle burn.

Fellow-citizens, I thank you for this opportunity to express the sentiments of the colored people of the South. [Applause.]

A MEMBER OF THE OHIO DELEGATION. Ohio was not silent in the war, but we have been silent in this great Convention. Now, we desire to be heard through a crippled soldier, General E. F. Noyes. [Great cheering, and calls for "Noyes!"]

Governor E. F. NOYES, of Ohio, speaking from his seat, said:

REMARKS OF GOVERNOR NOYES, OF OHIO.

Gentlemen of the Convention: I am exceedingly obliged to my enthusiastic friends for mentioning my name in this Convention, but I am confident that the delegates are now in no temper to listen to political speeches. [Cries of "Go on! go on!" during which the General was pushed forward to the stand by his friends.]

General NOYES, (resuming.) I certainly did not come here with any purpose of saying anything upon political subjects, and I am quite certain the feeling of our delegation is to talk less and work more. We don't want to stay here for another day. Many of the delegates have made their arrangements to go home, and we feel it is time to proceed with business. I am told that the Committee on Resolutions will not be able to report under two or three hours. If that is true it will be impossible for us to get through with the business of the Convention, and yet start home to-night. I hope the rules may be suspended, so that we can make these nominations, and then, when they are ready, let the Committee on Resolutions come in with their report.

I want now to say one word about Ohio, and then I am done. As the Governor of that State, I have been brought into somewhat intimate contact with all her people, and now I want to say to you for the State of Ohio, we shall be content with whatever nomination you make for Vice-President. We have a candidate of our own, a tried patriot and excellent gentleman, who, finding himself in the Cabinet of a recreant President, shook off the dust of his feet against him, not being willing to compromise or destroy the party that had honored him. [Applause.] We honor him; but let me say for Ohio that whoever shall be nominated here, you can count upon us to give a bigger majority than we gave four years ago. [Cheers.]

There is absolutely no disaffection in our State. [Renewed cheering.] A few prominent and excellent gentlemen, who are among my personal friends, identified themselves with what was known as the liberal movement, but every one of them of any prominence has become so heartily disgusted that they will vote for Grant now, if they would not before. [Great applause.] I asked a member of the Illinois delegation, who is a leading statesman, how it happened that in Cincinnati the Illinois delegation was the first to go over to Greeley. Said he, "We had the best set of men from any State, representative, leading men, and we were about equally divided between Davis and Trumbull, and when they could not be nominated, our delegation was determined to make the thing just as ridiculous as possible, retire, and go out." [Cheers and laughter.]

Now, we want to get at work. I hope the Convention will agree to go on and nominate our candidate for President, and if the committee are not ready, then the Vice-President; and then, if they are not ready, let us take a recess. [Cries of "Make the motion!"] I hardly like to do it. [Cries of "Make it!"] If the committee are ready after we have made the nomination, the report can come in. If, after we have done this, the committee are not ready, let us nominate our candidate for the Vice-Presidency, then, if need be, take a recess; but, for Heaven's sake, don't let us stay here and talk all day. [Cheers, and cries of "Make the motion!"]

Mr. President, I renew the motion to suspend the rules, and proceed first and only to the selection of our candidate for President. [Cheers.]

The motion was carried, amid great applause.

THE NOMINATION OF A CANDIDATE FOR PRESIDENT.

The Chairman announced the naming of candidates for President in order.

Mr. SHELBY M. CULLOM, of Illinois, having ascended the platform, said:

Gentlemen of the Convention: On behalf of the great Republican party of Illinois and that of the Union—in the name of liberty, of loyalty, of justice, and of law—

in the interest of economy, of good government, of peace, and of the equal rights of all—remembering with profound gratitude his glorious achievements in the field and his noble statesmanship as Chief Magistrate of this great nation—I NOMINATE AS PRESIDENT OF THE UNITED STATES, FOR A SECOND TERM, ULYSSES S. GRANT.

A scene of the wildest excitement followed this speech. The spacious Academy was crowded with thousands of spectators in every part; and on the stage, in the parquet, and in tier upon tier of galleries, arose deafening, prolonged, tumultuous cheers, swelling from pit to dome. A perfect wilderness of hats, caps, and handkerchiefs waved to and fro in a surging mass as three times three reverberated from the thousands of voices.

The band appeared to catch the prevailing enthusiasm, and waved their instruments as though they had been flags. Amid cries of "Music!" "Music!" they struck up "Hail to the Chief."

As the majestic stream of this music came floating down from the balcony, a life-size equestrian portrait of Grant came down as if by magic, filling the entire space of the back scene, and the enthusiasm knew no bounds.

Governor STEWART L. WOODFORD, of New York, then ascended the platform, and made the following address:

ADDRESS OF GOVERNOR WOODFORD, OF NEW YORK.

Mr. President and Gentlemen of the Convention: New York, the home of the distinguished editor who has been placed in nomination for the Presidency at Cincinnati, asks you to pause one moment before you record the formal nomination that is the prophecy of election, that she may reach out across the continent, strike hands with Illinois, and second the nomination of Ulysses S. Grant. [Cheers.] Seated by the sea, at the great eastern gateway of the continent, imperial in resources and in wealth, New York has the largest interest in the wisdom of your platform, in the integrity, the stability, and the fitness of your candidate. [Applause.]

Four years ago she sustained General Grant, because she recognized and would express the great debt of gratitude that the nation owed to the brave heart, the strong arm, and the silent lips of our great chieftain. To-day she endorses that nomination, because he has been tried and found faithful. When we have passed by the little quarrellings and criticisms of the hour, which are as the motes that float in the sunbeam, impartial history will wonder that the great Republic, through one of its recognized Senators of a Republican State, could have attempted to stain the sword and impeach the honor of the one man to whom, under God, the nation owes more than to any other. In his place upon the Senate floor the Senator from Massachusetts said it, and, as I read it according to the gospel of *The Tribune*, the text is probably correct.

He said that Stanton, just before he passed from earth, spoke thus:

"I know General Grant better than any other person in the country can know him. It was my duty to study him, and I did it, night and day, when I saw him and when I did not see him, and now I tell you what I know—he cannot govern this country."

Let the history of those perilous days reply that the great War Secretary indeed knew Grant through and through; that until the hour when Grant assumed personal command in Virginia, Stanton had been compelled to discharge not only his ministerial duties as Secretary, but to watch and guide the action of the commanders in the field; that from that hour he and Lincoln alike trusted, leaned upon, and confided in Grant, and left him free, according to his own judgment, to fight the rebellion in his own resolute and sure way.

Let history record that when our gallant Sherman seemed, in the judgment of the War Secretary, to have erred in the terms proposed for Johnston's surrender, that Stanton knew Grant so well that he sent him, all untried in diplomacy and statesmanship, to arrange the surrender and prevent possible legal complications and political misunderstandings. Let history also record that this plain soldier, of whose autocratic, egotistic, and imperial will the same Senator made such frequent mention, was so little disposed to assert himself, was so generous to the feelings of the great Lieutenant, that, having conferred with Sherman and indicated the purpose of the Government, and so prevented further possible mistakes, he left Sherman to complete the negotiation in his own name and by his own means. I challenge the records of the war and memories of his old soldiers to find one single instance where Grant ever sought to appropriate one single laurel that his comrade had gained, or failed to recognize and reward a comrade's merit and worth.

But to return. Stanton indeed knew Grant through and through. He knew that when for an hour Andrew Johnson may have meditated the use of force against the will of the people in Congress assembled, he did not dare to whisper his dream to Grant, but sought, by the creation of brevet ranks, to find others who might do his will. To the honor of the man and true men who stood that day in the highest rank, Johnson offered the commission in vain. Aye! Stanton knew Grant well. He knew that when, by assignment to the War Department *ad interim*, Grant filled for a time that high civic trust, the only barrier between the passion of the President and the renewal of civil strife was this patient, silent, loyal man, who, sound in peace as in war, was forever on the side of constitutional law, unity, and peace. Aye! he knew him well—so well, that during that long struggle, when Mr. Stanton stood and fought out the bitter fight between Presidential usurpation and Congressional authority, he leaned on Grant constantly and completely, and this Cæsar, whose red hand is to stop our liberty, was true at every time and in every place—as true to the people and the law as is the needle to the pole. Aye! Stanton knew Grant well; so well, that when he had been placed in nomination for the Presidency, Mr. Stanton pleaded for his election, endorsed his fitness, and labored for his success. These very walls still ring with the echo of that great speech, one of the last utterances of that great statesman in his own Pennsylvania—from the grave where he was killed from overwork in the Cabinet, as much a martyr to the war as though he had wasted in hospital or died on the field. His cold lips speak this day as in life. They spoke from this very platform. From the grave the dead Stanton rebukes the living Senator, and I hear his earnest and solemn approval of Ulysses S. Grant as soldier, man, and patriot.

In the name of millions of our loyal people, in the name of an enfranchised race, in the name of his old comrades, the living and the dead, in the name of the dead Secretary of War, New York endorses the nomination, and asks God's blessing on the cause. [Tremendous enthusiasm.]

Mr. M. D. BORUCK, of California, followed, and said:

ADDRESS OF M. D. BORUCK, OF CALIFORNIA.

Mr. President: Illinois rightly, in nominating Grant for re-election, claims him as her citizen. But, sir, though I come from a long distance, from that land where the setting sun lights up the peaceful waters of the Pacific, we claim, too, a portion of that citizenship which does such honor to Illinois. California, Oregon, and a portion of the Pacific slope, claim Grant as their honored citizen.

We have come, sir, a long distance to perform, it is true, a self-imposed duty in casting our votes for the greatest leader and greatest chieftain the world ever saw. We come, sir, if you please, from the land of the earthquake; and though like the wondrous rocking-stone reared by the Druids, which the finger of a child might vibrate to the centre, but which the might of armies could not move, so we stand there under those great convulsions of the earth; and, Mr. President, when the great convulsion of treason and rebellion and antagonism to our great and beloved country washed in frightful waves against her base, we stood there like rocks of adamant, unmoved and immovable. Sir, to be very brief, I desire to call the attention of this vast body to what I consider a remarkable coincidence in the words I shall name, differing, if you please, in but one small letter of the alphabet.

We all recollect that when the first gun was fired upon Fort Sumter, the loyal hearts of the people of the nation moved to the old flag and hastened to support it; and now, sir, with the first gun from Sumner, the loyal hearts of a nation rallies again to that standard held aloft by Grant, and in the contest which approaches in

November the same serried ranks will be presented, and a great victory will be achieved in his re-election. I promise you, sir, so far as the Pacific coast is concerned, to return a good account. [Long and continued applause.]

THE CALLING OF THE ROLL.

The PRESIDENT. The Secretary will call the roll of States, and each State will cast its vote.

The Secretary, Gen. H. H. BINGHAM, then called the list of States, and in response, the chairman of each State delegation announced the vote of his delegation, as follows :

ALABAMA.

E. M. KIELS, Chairman. I am instructed to cast the twenty votes of the Alabama delegation unanimously for that true, tried, great man, and model President, Ulysses S. Grant. [Applause.]

ARKANSAS.

POWELL CLAYTON, Chairman. I shall occupy so much of your time as to announce that the State of Arkansas gives her twelve votes for Ulysses S. Grant.

CALIFORNIA.

JAMES OTIS, Chairman. As chairman of the California delegation, I am instructed to cast her entire twelve votes for Ulysses S. Grant. [Applause.]

CONNECTICUT.

BARTLETT BENT, Chairman. To-day, as four years ago, Connecticut gives her twelve votes for Ulysses S. Grant.

DELAWARE.

J. R. LOFLAND, Chairman. I am instructed by the Delaware delegation to cast her six votes for Ulysses S. Grant.

FLORIDA.

DENNIS EAGAN, Chairman. The land of flowers gives her eight votes unanimously for Ulysses S. Grant.

GEORGIA.

J. S. BIGBY, Chairman. Georgia testifies her appreciation of a national Executive, and her gratitude for an administration that commands the approval of her people, by casting for Ulysses S. Grant twenty-two votes.

ILLINOIS.

S. M. CULLOM, Chairman. Illinois casts her forty-two votes for Ulysses S. Grant.

INDIANA.

HENRY S. LANE, Chairman. Indiana casts her thirty votes for Ulysses S. Grant.

IOWA.

GRENVILLE M. DODGE, Chairman. Iowa casts twenty-two votes for Ulysses S. Grant —all she has.

KANSAS.

BENJAMIN F. SIMPSON, Chairman. Kansas, first-born of the Republican party, desirous of serving four years longer under the same great chieftain, casts her ten votes for Ulysses S. Grant.

KENTUCKY.

WILLIAM C. GOODLOE, Chairman. Kentucky, that gave birth to Abraham Lincoln, casts twenty-four votes for his worthy successor, Ulysses S. Grant.

LOUISIANA.

JAMES LEWIS, Chairman. I am instructed by the sixteen delegates from my State in this Convention, and by the Republican party of my State, to cast the solid vote of Louisiana—sixteen votes—for Ulysses S. Grant.

MAINE.

ISAIAH STETSON, Chairman. Maine gives her grateful heart, and her fourteen votes, to Ulysses S. Grant.

MARYLAND.

JACOB TOME, Chairman. In accordance with the unanimous wishes and instructions of the convention which sent us as its delegates, and in complete unison with the feelings of every delegate here, and every member of the Republican party of Maryland, we cast her sixteen votes solid for Ulysses S. Grant.

MASSACHUSETTS.

GEORGE B. LORING, Chairman. Massachusetts casts her twenty-six votes for Ulysses S. Grant, and will give him thirteen votes in November next in the Electoral College.

MICHIGAN.

WILLIAM A. HOWARD, Chairman. Michigan has twenty-two delegates, and not an office-holder among them. We were sent here without any dictation from office-holders; we represent the Republican party of that State; we cast twenty-two votes for Ulysses S. Grant, and only wish we had forty-four to cast.

MINNESOTA.

D. M. SABIN, Chairman. The North Star proposes to spend all summer in fighting it out on this line. She gives her ten votes for Ulysses S. Grant.

MISSISSIPPI.

JAMES LYNCH, Chairman. Sixteen delegates from Mississippi request me to put that great State on national record as appreciating the wants of all this great country, as gratefully recognizing heroic and patriotic services, as pledged to maintain the liberty and political equality of all men, without regard to race or color, by nominating one for the Presidency of the United States whose connection with national affairs constitutes one of the brightest pages of the history of the Republic—President Ulysses S. Grant—for whom we cast her sixteen votes in this Convention.

NEBRASKA.

JOHN S. REDICK, Chairman. Nebraska gives her six votes for the tanner who will tan the hide of Horace in the vat of Democratic disunion, corruption, and damnation—Ulysses S. Grant.

NEVADA.

C. C. STEVENSON, Chairman. Nevada, born during the rebellion, admitted in time of strife, the silver State of the Union, casts her six votes for **Grant.**

NEW HAMPSHIRE.

FREDERICK SMYTH, Chairman. New Hampshire, one of the old thirteen States, and the birthplace of Horace Greeley, [laughter,] casts her vote for Ulysses S. Grant—ten votes, all she has—and she will give him her electoral vote in November.

NEW JERSEY.

CORTLANDT PARKER, Chairman. Determined to ratify her nomination in November, New Jersey, in gratitude for what her people deem a wise and pure administration, gives her eighteen votes for Ulysses S. Grant.

NEW YORK.

MARTIN I. TOWNSEND, Chairman. The Empire State, by the unanimous wish of her delegates, instructs me to cast her seventy votes for that man of whom it has been said by our distinguished fellow-citizen, Horace Greeley, he never has been beaten, and never will be—Ulysses S. Grant.

NORTH CAROLINA.

JOSEPH C. ABBOTT, Chairman. I am instructed by the delegates of North Carolina to say that the State called the Tar-heel State intends to stick to Ulysses S. Grant with her twenty votes. [Applause.]

OHIO.

SAMUEL CRAIGHEAD, Chairman. Ohio, the birthplace of Ulysses S. Grant, [applause,] presents her united front for this nomination to-day. Ohio, that never failed or faltered when Republican work was to be done—Ohio promises to this Convention and to the country 50,000 majority for the nominee. Ohio casts her united vote, forty-four in all, for Ulysses S. Grant.

OREGON.

J. F. DEVORE, Chairman. We are from the Sunset Land. We are happy to claim General Grant as a citizen of our State, and hence we are bound to second his nomination with six votes from Oregon.

PENNSYLVANIA.

MORTON MCMICHAEL, Chairman. (The appearance of Mr. McMichael on the platform was greeted with overwhelming demonstrations of applause.) After such a greeting I am without words. Pennsylvania, with her whole great heart, casts her fifty-eight votes for Ulysses S. Grant.

RHODE ISLAND.

AMBROSE E. BURNSIDE, Chairman. (The audience gave General Burnside three cheers as he rose to announce the vote of Rhode Island.) The Republican party of Rhode Island, the Republican convention of the State of Rhode Island, and all my brother delegates, have done me the honor of asking me to cast the entire vote of our State for my old comrade-in-arms, Ulysses S. Grant.

SOUTH CAROLINA.

E. W. M. MACKEY, Chairman. South Carolina, whose first hostile gun made Grant a possibility, has designated me, through her Republican delegation, to cast her vote in this Convention. Gazing upon the battered walls of old Sumter, mindful of the man whose triumphant sword opened her gates, marshaling two races within her border, South Carolina to-day, standing redeemed, regenerated, disenthralled, a State of law and order, casts her fourteen votes for Ulysses S. Grant.

TENNESSEE.

D. A. NUNN, Chairman. I am instructed by the delegates from the State of Tennessee, both white and colored, to cast her twenty-four votes for the most gallant soldier that the world ever saw, Ulysses S. Grant.

TEXAS.

WEBSTER FLANAGAN, Chairman. Texas, unlike any other State, was not permitted to take part in the late contest. To-day Texas claims the privilege of casting sixteen votes, and would like to have the privilege of casting thirty-two votes, and would that it were thirty-two thousand, for Ulysses S. Grant.

VERMONT.

J. GREGORY SMITH, Chairman. Vermont, as ever loyal, casts her ten votes for Ulysses S. Grant.

VIRGINIA.

John R. Popham, Chairman. Virginia casts her twenty-two votes for Ulysses S. Grant. She wishes she had as many hundreds to cast for him. As it is, she gives him all she has. It only remains for me to say that her patriotic, Republican people, inspired with the certain signs of approaching victory, marching under her proud banner, with her proud motto, "*Sic semper Tyrannis,*" mean, in the approaching campaign, to put their iron heel upon the tyrant Democratic head. Our cause is just, and Virginia must and shall be redeemed.

WEST VIRGINIA.

W. E. Stephenson, Chairman. West Virginia, following in the footsteps of her illustrious mother, casts her ten votes for Ulysses S. Grant.

WISCONSIN.

E. W. Keyes, Chairman. Wisconsin casts her twenty votes for Ulysses S. Grant.

ARIZONA.

John Titus, Chairman. Arizona casts two votes for Ulysses S. Grant.

COLORADO.

George M. Chillicothe, Chairman. Colorado casts two votes for Ulysses S. Grant.

DAKOTA.

Mr. Curtis, Chairman. Dakota, ward of the Government, casts her votes in this Convention as the only opportunity she has of voting for President. She casts these votes for the patriotic soldier, the soldier President, Ulysses S. Grant.

DISTRICT OF COLUMBIA.

John F. Cooke, Chairman. The District of Columbia, the seat of the United States government, has a desirable house to rent, desirable for habitation and much sought after. She desires that it shall be relet to the same tenant for another four years, and casts her two votes for Ulysses S. Grant.

IDAHO.

John R. McBride, Chairman. Idaho casts her vote in this Convention for Ulysses S. Grant, and only wishes she could vote for him in November.

NEW MEXICO.

Mr. Freeland, Chairman. New Mexico, occupying a humble position in this Convention, grateful for the privilege accorded to her, casts her two votes for Illinois' gifted son, wise in statesmanship, as he was gallant in war, Ulysses S. Grant.

UTAH.

A. S. Gould, Chairman. "On behalf of the loyal people of Utah, the delegation from that Territory thank God and this Convention for the privilege of casting her two little votes for Ulysses S. Grant, of whom it may be said as it was of another great and good man, "First in war, first in peace, and first in the hearts of his countrymen."

WASHINGTON.

Lyman B. Andrews, Chairman. Washington Territory, which has just cast off her swaddling-clothes, but who hopes hereafter to go full grown with you into the contest, casts her two votes for Ulysses S. Grant.

WYOMING.

J. W. Donnellan, Chairman. Wyoming, the last of the political organizations in America, is proud to cast its two votes for Ulysses S. Grant.

NATIONAL UNION REPUBLICAN CONVENTION,

THE BALLOT.

The ballot stood as follows:

	No. of Delegates.	For Grant.
Alabama	20	20
Arkansas	12	12
California	12	12
Connecticut	12	12
Delaware	6	6
Florida	8	8
Georgia	22	22
Illinois	42	42
Indiana	30	30
Iowa	22	22
Kansas	10	10
Kentucky	24	24
Louisiana	16	16
Maine	14	14
Maryland	16	16
Massachusetts	26	26
Michigan	22	22
Minnesota	10	10
Mississippi	16	16
Missouri	30	30
Nebraska	6	6
Nevada	6	6
New Hampshire	10	10
New Jersey	18	18
New York	70	70
North Carolina	20	20
Ohio	44	44
Oregon	6	6
Pennsylvania	58	58
Rhode Island	8	8
South Carolina	14	14
Tennessee	24	24
Texas	16	16
Vermont	10	10
Virginia	22	22
West Virginia	10	10
Wisconsin	20	20
Arizona	2	2
Colorado	2	2
Dakota	2	2
District of Columbia	2	2
Idaho	2	2
Montana	2	2
New Mexico	2	2
Utah	2	2
Washington	2	2
Wyoming	2	2
Total	752	752

THE RESULT.

The PRESIDENT, rising in his place, said: "It is a pleasure to the Chair to announce that Ulysses S. Grant has received 752 votes—the entire vote of every State and Territory in the Union."

The most tumultuous and continued cheering again burst from the immense audience.

The band, at this announcement, played the air of a "Grant Campaign Song," the tenor of which was sung by a gentleman standing among the instruments, and the chorus by a large choir of gentlemen. The song was received with great enthusiasm, and is as follows:

> Rally round our leaders, men,
> We're arming for the fight,
> We'll raise our glorious standard,
> And battle for the right.
> To swell our gallant army,
> Come from hill and plain,
> Grant shall win the victory
> For President again.
>
> *Chorus.*—Let the drum and bugle sound,
> We'll march to meet the foe;
> Let our joyous shouts resound
> That all the land may know,
> The sons of freedom in their might,
> Have come from hill and plain,
> To make the brave Ulysses
> Our President again.
>
> He's a gallant hero,
> And noble statesman, too,
> He's safely brought our Ship of State
> The darkest dangers through;
> Let every brave and true man
> Join our loyal band,
> Till loud resounds the victory
> From mountain, vale, and strand.
>
> *Chorus.*—Let the drum, &c.
>
> And when the battle's over,
> We homeward turn again,
> We'll join the lovely lasses
> To music's thrilling strain;
> And loud the anthem swelling,
> To Grant, our noble chief,
> Who won our country's battles,
> And saved the land from grief.
>
> *Chorus.*—Let the drum, &c.
>
> Then rally round our leaders, men,
> We're arming for the fight,
> We'll raise our glorious standard,
> And battle for the right.
> To swell our gallant army,
> Come from hill and plain,
> Grant shall win the victory
> For President again.
>
> *Chorus.*—Let the drum, &c.

When this was concluded, a cry went from the multitude, "John Brown!" The band struck up the familiar, electrifying strains which our soldiers used to sing when marching to the front. The whole concourse rose as one mass. From the parquet to the upper tier, the vast multitude stood up and rolled out the grand old hymn of freedom. Strong men wept with intensity of feeling. There was scarcely a dry eye in the great assemblage; not a heart that was not thrilled with the sublimity of the moment. When this song was at last finished, the cry came for "Rally Round the Flag," and the air of that battle-song was given by the band, the whole audience singing the words with the same fervor with which the hymn had been rendered. This concluded, the band gave "Yankee Doodle," in the midst of tumultuous cheers.

Lucius B. Church, of Montana, was then loudly called for, and in response ascended the platform. He said:

REMARKS OF LUCIUS B. CHURCH.

Ladies and Gentlemen of the Convention: Twelve years ago, in the wigwam at Chicago, preparatory to the nomination of Mr. Lincoln, I was called upon for a patriotic song. My selection at that time was our army and navy song, "The Red, White, and Blue." If there are any here who were present at that time they will remember the spontaneous chorus we had. I will ask the indulgence of the band and of that choir to play the first stanzas of "The Red, White, and Blue," in order that we may get the key correctly, and then I will sing the solo, inviting you to join in the chorus.

The band then played the air as requested, and the song was rendered with great effect, the audience joining in the chorus.

Calls were then made, loud and continuous, for "Marching through Georgia." Mr. CHURCH complied, and the audience, standing, again joined in the chorus.

When the song was completed, Mr. CHURCH said: "Now I ask for three cheers for those loyal black men who stood by us during that march through Georgia to the sea."

The cheers were given with great enthusiasm.

NOMINATION OF VICE-PRESIDENT.

Mr. CRAIGHEAD, of Ohio. *Mr. President:* Inasmuch as a very large number of the delegates who are here are anxious to discharge all the duties for which they have come together, and as I see no reason why we should not proceed to do those duties which remain to be discharged, I move you that the rules be suspended again, and that we proceed to the nomination of the candidate for the Vice-Presidency of the United States. [Great applause.]

The motion was agreed to.

The PRESIDENT. Nominations for Vice-President are now in order.

HENRY WILSON, OF MASSACHUSETTS, PROPOSED.

The Hon. MORTON MCMICHAEL, of Pennsylvania, appeared upon the stage, and said:

Mr. President: I beg your indulgence, and the indulgence of the Convention, for a few moments, preparatory to making nomination of a candidate for Vice-President of the United States. I do not come here, sir, for the purpose of uttering needless complaint; but I do feel that there is a complaint for me to make. Sir, the Republican party had both its birth and its baptism on Pennsylvania soil. At Pittsburgh it was called into existence by voluntary gathering, and in Philadelphia it received the solemn sanction of the people, and from the hour of its organization to this, Pennsylvania has always steadfastly upheld the principles upon which it was founded. You, sir, and all who hear me, remember it, and when, because of the successes of those principles, the South plunged madly into revolt, and with formidable martial preparations challenged the North to mortal combat, Pennsylvania was the first in the field and foremost in the fight. [Great applause.]

God forbid, sir, that by even so much as a fragment of a syllable I should utter any sound derogatory to the gallant and noble spirits who at the signal-gun of the war, from rolling prairie and rushing river, from the silence of the forest and the depths of the mine, from the glow of the furnace, from the din of the factory, and from the bustle of the mart, from church and college, swarmed to the defence of the national capital. But ours was the border-land of the war. Hence, it was our distinction to be the first at the scene of peril and to bring glad tidings of the rescue. In all the troubled hours that followed, Pennsylvania never grew weary or shirked her duty. By regiments, by brigades, by divisions, aye, sir, by armies of soldiers, she came to the rescue, and from her tax-burdened exchequer thousands, tens of thousands, hundreds of thousands, and millions, she gave to sustain the cause. In the supreme council of the nation foremost, she was heard among the earnest, the clearest, and the loudest in aid of that grandest of all grand Republican achievement—the emancipation of four million of human souls from a bondage worse than death.

I ask you, sir, how has Pennsylvania been requited? Four years ago she presented to the Convention at Chicago her famous war Governor as a candidate for Vice-President, and he was rejected. But, though disappointed, she never murmured. In the conflict that followed, she engaged with all her energies in behalf of the Republican nominees. They were elected, and from that time forward what State has stood so earnestly by the National Administration or the Republican party on all questions of distinctive policy? Her delegation in Congress—the Republican members, of course, I mean—have been their staunchest adherents; yet, when these same members have ventured to urge that her interests, in common with those of the whole country, shall not be overlooked, she is denounced as selfish, her people are maligned, and her motives are misrepresented. I trust that before this Convention adjourns it will declare, and that with no uncertain voice, its adherence to those cardinal, economic doctrines which are the very life of our life—our fidelity to the interests and the rights of all sections, North and South, East and West, alike.

I hesitate to continue the catalogue of complaint; but it is painful to acknowledge that this mighty Commonwealth for years has been imploring that her metropolis, second in population and first in industrial activities in this country, should be allowed some suitable arrangement for its post office, and it is only within a few days that her prayer has been grudgingly granted.

It is humiliating to be obliged to confess that for years she has been beseeching that the unrivalled naval station, which, as it now appears, with improvident generosity she bestowed on the nation, might be adequately improved, and that it still lies waste and neglected. Sir, when the great public offices of the country are to be filled, she is disregarded. In the Cabinet at Washington she has no voice; in the most important foreign missions she has no representatives. And yet, sir, when recently a journal dedicated to her service proposed that, for reasons similar to those I have mentioned, it might be expedient to select one of her citizens as Vice-President, the proposition was met with sneers, and in one conspicuous instance with worse than sneers—with the insolent declaration, "Pennsylvania, as usual, comes forward with the demand, looking as much like a threat as a demand, about Presidential candidates."

Now I say, sir, that it is utterly untrue that Pennsylvania ever made any demand on such a subject. It would have been, perhaps, far better for her had she done so. It would have been better for her had she insisted upon the position which her rank, her strength, and her influence entitled her to, but which she did not then and does not now demand. And for the purpose of showing how utterly unfounded are all imputations against her, as feeling jealousy or animosity toward her sister States, I will say that this offensive paragraph to which I have referred appeared in a paper printed and circulated in the city of Boston.

And now, as a fitting reply to the insinuations that that paper contained, I am here, under the unanimous instructions of the Pennsylvania delegation, to present the name of a statesman known to the country as an honest, upright, able man, who has labored, and is laboring still, earnestly in behalf of the laboring masses of the country, and for the good of the whole country; I mean Henry Wilson, of Massachusetts. [Mr. McMichael closed amid the wildest applause.]

Mr. LORING, of Massachusetts, came forward to the platform, and said:

SPEECH OF DR. LORING, OF MASSACHUSETTS.

Mr. President and Gentlemen of the Convention: I have but one word to say, gentlemen, upon this subject. Massachusetts has not occupied much of the time of the Convention in speech-making. She has sat here silently and quietly, ready that her voice should be heard whenever called for, and ready to do her duty in solid column when the occasion demands it. I desire to say to this Convention that there is no division in the Republican party in Massachusetts so far as the Administration of General Grant is concerned. [Applause.] I desire, in behalf of that Commonwealth, so true, so devoted to republican principles, to express the gratitude of the delegation from that State to the gentleman who has put in nomination her favorite Senator and son.

Mr. President, this is not the first time that Pennsylvania and Massachusetts have stood side by side. The gentleman who has addressed you said that republicanism found its birth and baptism in Pennsylvania. So they did; but in those days Massachusetts sent down here her John Adams, and Samuel Adams; the blood of Warren and General Hancock gave birth to the cause of republicanism; and if it is true that in 1776 republicanism was baptized on this soil, it is also true that Massachusetts was here, and stood by the cradle on that occasion.

Now, I desire to second the nomination of the gentleman from Pennsylvania. In presenting the name of Henry Wilson as a candidate for the Vice-Presidency of the United States, he has not only paid a tribute to the fidelity of Massachusetts to republicanism, but he has paid a tribute to that spirit of genius, ·devotion, fidelity, honesty, and honor which will always pave the way to great success to the poor and toiling in this country. [Applause.]

Henry Wilson represents, in all his attributes, more than any man I know of, the power of high principles, of thorough devotion, to overcome all the obstacles which fall in the path of childhood, and youth, and mature years. For more than a quarter of a century, he has adhered to the great principles of this party. He was devoted to them long before it was a party, and when Massachusetts stood almost alone in the great cause, it was Henry Wilson whose voice was early heard in the cause of freedom. I ask you to name to me the commonwealth in this Union where that voice has not been heard in the cause. I ask you to point me the down-trodden and oppressed citizens of the United States who have not been encouraged by Henry Wilson, and aided in lifting themselves above the oppressor. [Applause.] I ask, moreover, the successful politicians of this, and of almost every State, to tell me how many times Henry Wilson's voice has been heard speaking for them and their cause. [Applause.] Warm-hearted, generous, devoted to the Republican principles of brotherhood, this land over, he is ready to do his duty in season and out of season. And let me tell you, my friends, that as Henry Wilson stood by the cradle of the Republican party in his poverty and in his youth, he, if this party is to fall, will follow it to the grave, the saddest and most broken-hearted mourner in all that mournful procession. He is devoted to this cause, and I assure you that he will add strength to the ticket put in nomination to-day, representing, as he does, the toiling people of this country. [Applause.]

Mr. OSSIAN RAY, of New Hampshire, spoke as follows:

SPEECH OF OSSIAN RAY.

Gentlemen of the Convention: Coming as I do from the State in which Henry Wilson was born, it gives me unbounded pleasure to announce that we are united on Massachusetts' favorite and great Senator, Henry Wilson. [Applause.] We ought to nominate him as Vice-President because he is a good man and true, because he has always been the friend of the people, whose instincts and impulses are always right. It is peculiarly appropriate we should honor ourselves by honoring him with the nomination. It is as fitting a disapproval on the part of the Republican party of the course of his colleague as could be given. [Applause.]

Another reason why I think he should be nominated on this ticket is that I firmly believe if we were to call up the entire nation and have its vote taken throughout the land, he would receive the entire vote of the Republican party. If they could decide whether or not Henry Wilson should be nominated or some other man selected as a candidate, he would carry the day by a million majority. [Prolonged cheers.] We are here simply to register the choice of the people. The name of Henry Wilson is one which will add strength and fame even to that of the colossal name of the great Captain of the Western World. [Applause.]

Like General Grant, he has been the architect of his own fortunes. He commenced life poor, by graduating from a shoemaker's shop. It is the pride and glory of American civilization that by industry, honesty, and perseverance the highest offices within the nation's gift are within the possible reach of the humblest youth in the land. With a good tanner at the head of the ticket to tan the pelts of the enemy, and with a good shoemaker to sew them up, and drive the pegs, if need be, we shall win next November by a large majority. I pray you, gentlemen, **to nominate the honest and noble Henry Wilson.** [Cheers.]

NAME OF SCHUYLER COLFAX PRESENTED.

Mr. RICHARD W. THOMPSON, of Indiana, addressed the Convention as follows:

In behalf of the united Republican party of the State of Indiana, and in obedience to the unanimous instructions of our State convention, in behalf of the delegates of the State of Indiana, I am instructed to nominate the Hon. Schuyler Colfax. [Prolonged applause.] I do this with satisfaction, because it is a just reward of eminent ability and devoted public service, [cheers,] of devotion to the country and the integrity and honor of the Union; but that satisfaction is somewhat alloyed by the fact that we find our older and better sister of Massachusetts presenting one of her eminent and honored sons, for whom we have the highest possible respect. [Cheers.]

If Mr. Colfax were a new man, I should be required to tell you who and what he was. He is not unknown to fame. Four years ago the names of Grant and Colfax were associated together. [Cheers.] They were the battle-cry which led to that great triumph, placing the principles of reconstruction prominently before the world, emblazoned on the flag of the Republican party. [Cheers.] We do not think they should be separated until another triumph has been won. [Cheers.] We do not think the partnership should be now dissolved, because the firm is not yet insolvent, and its assets are not yet ready to be turned over to the hands of a receiver. [Cheers.] We, however, desire to say upon this question, and to be distinctly understood, that we have no antagonism with our older sisters, Massachusetts and Pennsylvania.

For every man of the delegation which I represent, and for myself personally, I say that among the men of this country who have stood forth boldly in defence of the life of the nation, those who represent the purity of our national institutions, there is not one more worthy to be received with honor than Henry Wilson, of Massachusetts. [Applause.] And in that respect he is not unlike Schuyler Colfax. [Renewed applause.] Without the aid of adventitious wealth in early life, they have both carved their way to eminence and distinction. They have been enabled to reach the highest positions of honor and distinction in the land, and whether the Republican party shall place the name of one or the other upon the standard which is to bear the name of Grant, it will have achieved a triumph. The honor of the nation may be trusted with them both.

But, while Massachusetts and Pennsylvania, elder sisters of ours, were true to the principles of liberty and of the Republican party, they should not forget that we in the West, younger than they, have followed their example; that when the tocsin of war was sounded, when the flag of rebellion was unfurled, the West was not behind its older sisters in pouring out its treasure and the blood of its sons for the maintenance of the integrity of the Union. [Applause.]

Feeling, therefore, as we do, that by joining the name of Colfax with that of Grant, we utter the same old battle-cry which has been repeated by every child in the land—"Grant and Colfax"—and that it will be the signal of victory, we present his name. [Applause.] We urge his name, believing, as we do, that with it upon our flag, our own State will be triumphant, our party throughout the Union will be triumphant, and the work of reconstruction finally completed, so that hereafter there shall be no more talk of compromise between the extremes of parties, no sugar-coated pills of liberalism and democracy to be administered to our people as the cure for all national ills, but that our nation, going forward in a grand career of glory, will become what she is destined to be, the great shining light of the world, from which shall go out the true principles of republicanism to lead other nations to triumph and victory with us. [Prolonged cheering.]

Mr. WILLIAM A. HOWARD, of Michigan, was then loudly called for, and upon taking the stand spoke as follows:

SPEECH OF WILLIAM A. HOWARD, OF MICHIGAN.

Mr. President and Gentlemen of the Convention: I represent that State which first perfected a Republican State organization—that State which first applied the name to a State organization, with all due deference to my friend from Pennsylvania. The oak tree still stands where that organization was made. No Senator from any State who is now living was there to receive applause when the name was uttered. Whether there will be any Senator to follow the hearse remains to be seen. In the border of that State, before the State had a name, there came a stripling youth from the great Empire State of New York. He located within five miles of our border. In a little room he opened a printing office. He was compositor, pressman, and editor, and before he was of age, in that way he supported a mother and built up his business, developed his intellect, cultivated statesmanship, and is now the second officer in the great United States. [Applause.]

Eight years ago—yes, ten years ago—when the war was raging, he was made the presiding officer of the popular branch of this great government. So steadily did he hold the reins, with such exact justice did he administer parliamentary law, so firmly did he support the Union, that with his present associate, General Grant, in the field, the war proved a success. Four years ago his name was associated with that of General Grant on the Presidential ticket. Grant and Colfax became the rallying cry throughout the land. Both have proved eminently faithful and successful. In God's name, we ask, why should these names to-day be separated? We do not appeal to this Convention in behalf of our State. Thank God, she stands on her own Republican devotion. With our choice we will ring in a good old twenty thousand majority.

And in passing, let me say that I accord with all that has been said of the son of Massachusetts. I know him well. I have seen him in those days that tried men's souls. I glory with Massachusetts in her honored son. But I pray you, gentlemen, do not endanger a doubtful State by insulting her noble son. Insult, did I say? That is too strong an expression. There is not a man in this Convention who would willingly insult Schuyler Colfax. Not one; but it might imply censure. We feel more tenderly for him than if he were a citizen of our own State. Gather up all the good qualities of the candidate named from Massachusetts, and we concede them all, and Schuyler Colfax matches every one of them. He represents a State which may be doubtful, but in which success is certain with his name combined with that of the great leader.

Now, gentlemen of the Convention, I have just one word, and I will relieve your patience. I think the Republican party have a right to appeal to the work that has been done and to name the men who have done it. And, sir, if the good old Roman matron once made her name immortal by pointing to her children, when asked to show her jewels, I say that the Republican party occupies a prouder position to-day than any man or party has occupied since the world began. We present as our jewels four millions of people, whom we found with the shackles of slavery upon them. We found them in shackles, and we present them here before the American people as four millions of free, independent citizens, enjoying all the rights of any favored citizens.

These are our jewels, and therefore I say we have a right to appeal to justice in behalf of those men who have accomplished these great results. Gentlemen of the Convention, I beg leave to say in conclusion, without one word of detraction from any candidate who has been named here—I would take him to my heart of hearts if I deemed it a new question—yet I am constrained, in behalf of the united delegation from a State that never faltered one step from the beginning of the organization, to second the nomination of Schuyler Colfax, of Indiana.

Mr. LYNCH, of Mississippi, said:

SPEECH OF MR. LYNCH, OF MISSISSIPPI.

Mr. President: It seems to me that at this important moment the spirit of the martyred President, whose name is written in every heart, rests upon me, and I remember his words on one occasion, that "it was not safe to swap horses while crossing a stream." [Cheers.] I cannot forget the calamity we experienced once by making a swap similar to the one proposed. Now, the name of the gentleman (Mr. Wilson) who has been nominated by other friends is also great. His career, too, is noble. He will be remembered wherever unsullied patriotism and noble devotion to liberty and equality shall be cherished by the people of this country. But I rise to support the nomination of one who stands forth, also, one of the highest symbols of American patriotism and American virtue, whose greatness of mind and goodness of heart causes him to glow with that magnetic power which touches the heart of every man, woman, and child in this great land of ours—Schuyler Colfax. [Prolonged applause.]

SPEECH OF GERRIT SMITH.

Mr. GERRIT SMITH, of New York, next addressed the Convention. He spoke in high terms of Mr. Colfax, and also of General Hawley, who was prominently before them as a candidate. But his preference was for Henry Wilson, an old abolitionist, whose first vote for President was for James G. Birney, and who had ever been the faithful friend and able advocate of the laboring man. His own early life was one of poverty and toil. Mr. Colfax's living in a State adjoining General Grant's Mr. Smith regarded as no small objection to Mr. Colfax's nomination.

Mr. CORTLANDT PARKER, of New Jersey, succeeded Mr. Smith. He said, in substance:

In conformity with the wish of New Jersey, expressed by her convention, and speaking the unanimous voice of her delegation, and at their request, I trespass on the patience of the Convention with a few words in behalf of Schuyler Colfax. Not that either we or our people yield to any in appreciation of the distinguished merits of Henry Wilson. Between two such men it is hard to choose. The pride which, as Republicans, we have in possessing them, becomes almost sorrow when such a choice is necessary. Both are eminently representative men. They are each the product of Republican principles. Both are of the people, lovers of right, lovers, in all things, of their country. Both have dignified every office they have filled. Both will adorn any station to which they may be elevated. But the people of New Jersey ask why, when the country says to Ulysses S. Grant, "Well done, good and faithful servant," the same should not be said to Schuyler Colfax. Of him it may be truly said that not one of his official acts has ever been criticised, much less reprehended, and if so untoward an event should occur as the death of the President, the world would still confide in the stability of our institutions, did their maintenance fall into the hands of Colfax as our Executive. Nor should locality be urged against him, for the man of Indiana is no longer a western man; the West lies hundreds of miles beyond. Indiana has become a central State. New Jersey clings, then, to her first choice—her choice of four years ago—Schuyler Colfax, of Indiana.

Mr. J. F. QUARLES, of Georgia, said:

REMARKS OF MR. QUARLES, OF GEORGIA.

Gentlemen of the Convention: I arise on behalf of a large portion of the Georgia delegation, and on behalf of a great majority of the Southern Republicans, to second the nomination of Henry Wilson, of Massachusetts. [Applause.] While much honor is due to Schuyler Colfax, after all, this great champion of human liberty and freedom in this country deserves something at the hands of the American people. [Applause.]

Sir, commencing his early life in poverty, he began almost with his manhood the battles of humanity in this country. Massachusetts has repeatedly honored him, as she ought to have done; but his reputation is broader than the State of Massachusetts. It reaches out further than any State line can extend, and embraces his whole country. [Applause.] He has labored for his country earnestly and long. He has fought long and well in behalf of human liberty, American honor and dignity, and we think the time has come when the people of this country should give him a recognition for his services. [Applause.] We of the South have an especial interest in this matter. We remember the fiery ordeal through which we have passed, and we remember that while bold and true men stood by us in that ordeal Henry Wilson was among the foremost.

With all due deference to the gentleman who has spoken upon the opposite side of this question, we say that it is always safe to swap horses anywhere if we get one equally as good. [Applause.] Sir, we hold that this is due, not only to the services of Henry Wilson, but that it is due especially to Massachusetts and to the East. [Applause. Cries of "Good! good!"] We have taken our President again and again from the West. The Republican party has never selected a candidate for the Presidency from the East. We have taken our Vice-President at the last election from the West, and we hold that some recognition is due to the East for its devotion to the country. [Cries of "Good!"]

Mr. Chairman, then, in behalf of much the larger portion of the Georgia delegation, in behalf of the great loyal heart of the people of the South, it gives me inexpressible pleasure to second the nomination of the Hon. Henry Wilson, of Massachusetts. [Great applause.]

THE NAME OF JOHN F. LEWIS, OF VIRGINIA, PRESENTED.

Mr. JAMES B. SENER, of Virginia, next addressed the Convention. He said:

I ask ten minutes for Virginia, not for myself, but for others. We come here to-day, a representative delegation from Virginia, to express the preference of the Republican party in that State in this Convention. We are here by the grace of God and the Republican party of Virginia, and I tell you, men of all sections, men of the North, men of the South, men of the East, and men of the West, that we who in the South endured the fires of the rebellion have the right to be heard.

Mr. President, if God has taught me anything in the history of the civil war it is this: that the North and the South, although divided for awhile, like the waters of the Mississippi may again mingle and flow on in harmony. The Republican party, representing all these diverse channels of human freedom and civil liberty, is yet a unit. Whoever speaks the principles of that party speaks for Virginia.

So great confusion now prevailed as to make the voice of the speaker wholly inaudible. He closed by placing in nomination, in behalf of the Virginia delegation, John F. Lewis, of that State, as a suitable candidate for Vice-President of the United States; a man who, when the fires of rebellion stirred all hearts, was true in his patriotism and devotion to the Union; a man on whose skirts there rest none of the taints of civil war; a man who has been true to the Constitution. "I ask you," said the speaker, "now, men of the North and men of the South, in the name of constitutional liberty and of constitutional law, to rise equal to this great occasion and endorse the nomination I make of John F. Lewis, of Virginia."

THE NAME OF E. J. DAVIS, OF TEXAS, PRESENTED.

Mr. FLANNAGAN, of Texas, next spoke from a portion of the hall distant from the platform, and was nearly inaudible.

He said that while paying due respect to the great names presented to this Convention for the second office in the gift of the American people, endorsing them all as fit and proper men, he presented one whose name stands high in all the States of this Union among all those who love right and justice, a man known and honored among all loyal men of his own State—in the name of the hundred thousand loyal, true-hearted men of Texas—the name of Governor E. J. Davis, of that State.

THE NAME OF HORACE MAYNARD, OF TENNESSEE, PRESENTED.

Mr. DAVID A. NUNN, of Tennessee, also speaking from the audience, was heard indistinctly.

He said he was instructed by the delegation from Tennessee to place in nomination a name not unknown to the people of this nation, the name of a man whose reputation is co-extensive with the Union; eminent in the councils of the nation; a son of the noble and proud old Commonwealth of Massachusetts by birth and education, a citizen of the gallant State of Tennessee by adoption and forty years' residence, combining the elements of both North and South; a man who, in the dark hour of the nation's trouble, never faltered, but stood unmovable as the granite hills. He was at the head of the party in Tennessee that crushed out Andrew Johnson when he proved false to that party, that crushed out the Democracy and struck the death-blow to Ku-Kluxism. That man was Horace Maynard.

THE PLATFORM.

The PRESIDENT announced that the Committee on Resolutions were now ready to report, and asked whether the business in which the Convention was engaged should be suspended for that purpose.

General assent was expressed by the Convention.

Mr. SCOFIELD, of Pennsylvania, chairman of the Committee on Resolutions, then said:

The Committee on Resolutions are now prepared to report a platform. Governor Hawley, of Connecticut, who acted as secretary to the committee, will read the report. I beg gentlemen to remember, as it is read, that the committee had but a very short time to consider a great number of subjects which were presented; and that while every gentleman may not find in our report everything he may desire, it will be observed that the committee have shown no disposition to avoid any question which is agitating the country at the present time. The committee have not been content to repose, as perhaps they might have done, upon the laurels of the party, and refer simply to its past record, but have made expression upon all the great questions of the day. I will not detain the Convention, because you are all anxious to hear what has been done. We submit it now, from the lips of Governor Hawley, to your judgment.

Governor HAWLEY then read the resolutions, as follows:

The Republican party of the United States, assembled in National Convention in the city of Philadelphia, on the 5th and 6th days of June, 1872, again declares its faith, appeals to its history, and announces its position upon the questions before the country.

First. During eleven years of supremacy it has accepted with grand courage the solemn duties of the time. It suppressed a gigantic rebellion, emancipated four millions of slaves, decreed the equal citizenship of all, and established universal suffrage. Exhibiting unparalleled magnanimity, it criminally punished no man for political offences, and warmly welcomed all who proved loyalty by obeying the laws and dealing justly with their neighbors. It has steadily decreased with a firm hand the resultant disorders of a great war, and initiated a wise and humane policy toward the Indians. The Pacific railroad and similar vast enterprises have been generously aided and successfully conducted, the public lands freely given to actual settlers, immigration protected and encouraged, and a full acknowledgment of the naturalized citizen's rights secured from European Powers. A uniform national currency has been provided, repudiation frowned down, the national credit sustained under the most extraordinary burdens, and new bonds negotiated at lower rates. The revenues have been carefully collected and honestly applied. Despite large annual reductions of the rates of taxation, the public debt has been reduced during General Grant's Presidency at the rate of a hundred millions a year, great financial crises have been avoided, and peace and plenty prevail throughout the land. Menacing foreign difficulties have been peacefully and honorably composed, and the honor and power of the nation kept in high respect throughout the world. This glorious record of the past is the party's best pledge for the future. We believe the people will not entrust the Government to any party or combination of men composed chiefly of those who have resisted every step of this beneficent progress.

Second. The recent amendments to the national Constitution should be cordially sustained because they are right, not merely tolerated because they are laws, and should be carried out according to their spirit by appropriate legislation, the enforcement of which can safely be entrusted only to the party that secured those amendments.

Third. Complete liberty and exact equality in the enjoyment of all civil, political, and public rights should be established and effectually maintained throughout the Union by efficient and appropriate State and Federal legislation. Neither the law nor its administration should admit any discrimination in respect of citizens by reason of race, creed, color, or previous condition of servitude.

Fourth. The National Government should seek to maintain honorable peace with all nations, protecting its citizens everywhere, and sympathizing with all peoples who strive for greater liberty.

Fifth. Any system of the civil service under which the subordinate positions of the Government are considered rewards for mere party zeal is fatally demoralizing, and we therefore favor a reform of the system by laws which shall abolish the evils of patronage, and make honesty, efficiency, and fidelity the essential qualifications for public positions, without practically creating a life-tenure of office.

Sixth. We are opposed to further grants of the public lands to corporations and monopolies, and demand that the national domain be set apart for free homes for the people.

Seventh. The annual revenue, after paying current expenditures, pensions, and the interest on the public debt, should furnish a moderate balance for the reduction of the principal, and that revenue, except so much as may be derived from a tax upon tobacco and liquors, should be raised by duties upon importations, the details of which should be so adjusted as to aid in securing remunerative wages to labor, and to promote the industries, prosperity, and growth of the whole country.

Eighth. We hold in undying honor the soldiers and sailors whose valor saved the Union. Their pensions are a sacred debt of the nation, and the widows and orphans of those who died for their country are entitled to the care of a generous and grateful people. We favor such additional legislation as will extend the bounty of the Government to all our soldiers and sailors who were honorably discharged, and who, in the line of duty, became disabled, without regard to the length of service or the cause of such discharge.

Ninth. The doctrine of Great Britain and other European powers concerning allegiance—"once a subject always a subject"—having at last, through the efforts of the Republican party, been abandoned, and the American idea of the individual's right to transfer allegiance having been accepted by European nations, it is the duty of our Government to guard with jealous care the rights of adopted citizens against the assumption of unauthorized claims by their former governments; and we urge continued careful encouragement and protection of voluntary immigration.

Tenth. The franking privilege ought to be abolished, and the way prepared for a speedy reduction in the rates of postage.

Eleventh. Among the questions which press for attention is that which concerns the relations of capital and labor, and the Republican party recognizes the duty of so shaping legislation as to secure full protection and the amplest field for capital, and for labor—the creator of capital—the largest opportunities and a just share of the mutual profits of these two great servants of civilization.

Twelfth. We hold that Congress and the President have only fulfilled an imperative duty in their measures for the suppression of violent and treasonable organizations in certain lately rebellious regions, and for the protection of the ballot-box, and therefore they are entitled to the thanks of the nation.

Thirteenth. We denounce repudiation of the public debt, in any form or disguise, as a national crime. We witness with pride the reduction of the principal of the debt, and of the rates of interest upon the balance, and confidently expect that our excellent national currency will be perfected by a speedy resumption of specie payment.

Fourteenth. The Republican party is mindful of its obligations to the loyal women of America for their noble devotion to the cause of freedom. Their admission to wider fields of usefulness is viewed with satisfaction, and the honest demand of any class of citizens for additional rights should be treated with respectful consideration.

Fifteenth. We heartily approve the action of Congress in extending amnesty to those lately in rebellion, and rejoice in the growth of peace and fraternal feeling throughout the land.

Sixteenth. The Republican party proposes to respect the rights reserved by the people to themselves as carefully as the powers delegated by them to the State and to the Federal Government. It disapproves of the resort to unconstitutional laws for the purpose of removing evils, by interference with rights not surrendered by the people to either the State or National Government.

Seventeenth. It is the duty of the general Government to adopt such measures as may tend to encourage and restore American commerce and shipbuilding.

Eighteenth. We believe that the modest patriotism, the earnest purpose, the sound judgment, the practical wisdom, the incorruptible integrity, and the illustrious services of Ulysses S. Grant have commended him to the heart of the American people, and with him at our head we start to-day upon a new march to victory.

Nineteenth. Henry Wilson, nominated for the Vice-Presidency, known to the whole land from the early days of the great struggle for liberty as an indefatigable laborer in all campaigns, an incorruptible legislator and representative man of

American institutions, is worthy to associate with our great leader and share the honors which we pledge our best efforts to bestow upon them.

The nineteenth resolution was adopted after the nomination of Vice-President.

General BURNSIDE, of Rhode Island. *Mr. President:* I move the adoption of the platform as a whole.

The motion was put, and unanimously carried.

NOMINATION OF VICE-PRESIDENT.

The Convention then resumed the business which was suspended to receive the report of the Committee on Resolutions, it being the execution of the order that the Convention now proceed to nominate a candidate for Vice-President.

A DELEGATE from Virginia. *Mr. President:* It is with reluctance that I am compelled to ask the attention of the Convention for a moment, but the instructions which the delegates from Virginia have received from an honest constituency impel me to ask your attention. An honorable gentleman, a representative of the Virginia delegation, took the stand a few minutes ago, and claimed that there was not due courtesy paid him while placing in nomination John F. Lewis. For this reason I am compelled to say to this Convention that while I am individually in favor of Henry Wilson, of Massachusetts, I desire now under instructions also to propose the name of Mr. John F. Lewis for the Vice-Presidency.

Governor NOYES, of Ohio, then being called upon, took the stand, and said:

SPEECH OF GOVERNOR NOYES.

Mr. President: On behalf of a large majority of the Ohio delegation; on behalf of a large Republican constituency which they represent; on behalf of the colored people, whose best friend I shall shortly name—the best friend in those days when there were few; in the name of our living soldiers, and in the name of my dead comrades who sleep upon the Southern battle-fields, I should fail in my duty if I did not second the nomination of the Hon. Henry Wilson, of Massachusetts. [Great applause.]

REMARKS OF MR. BICKHAM, OF OHIO.

Mr. BICKHAM, of Ohio. *Mr. President:* In behalf of a very large and very respectable minority of the Ohio delegation, who have just as many claims upon the soldiers and the negroes as the majority, I would fail in my duty if I did not present the claims of the Hon. Schuyler Colfax. [Applause.]

REMARKS OF MR. HILL, OF MISSISSIPPI.

Mr. HILL, of Mississippi. *Mr. President:* In behalf of a majority of my delegation, I wish to state to this Convention that we are in favor of Henry Wilson, of Massachusetts. While I regret that Mr. Colfax wrote his letter withdrawing from the candidacy for Vice-President, I cannot change with him, now that he is running for the nomination, or with anybody else.

REMARKS OF GOVERNOR CLAYTON.

Governor POWELL CLAYTON, of Arkansas. *Mr. President:* Four years ago, at Chicago, the Republican delegation from Arkansas threw a unanimous vote for Henry Wilson, of Massachusetts, as candidate for Vice-President, and time has only strengthened the devotion of the Republicans of our State for that great and good man. The name of Henry Wilson is as common as a household word in every hamlet throughout the South, and will be supported by our delegation with the solid vote of Arkansas in this Convention. In saying this I am not to be understood as detracting in any word or syllable from the bright and glorious record of that great statesman now occupying the chair of the Vice-President. [Cries of "Vote! vote!"]

The PRESIDENT. If there are no more nominations to be made, the Secretary will call the roll.

The roll of States was then called by the Secretary, and at the conclusion of the roll-call the vote stood as follows:

NATIONAL UNION REPUBLICAN CONVENTION,

THE BALLOT FOR VICE-PRESIDENT.

At the conclusion of the roll-call the vote stood as follows:

	No. of Delegates.	Henry Wilson, of Massachusetts.	Schuyler Colfax, of Indiana.	Horace Maynard, of Tennessee.	John F. Lewis, of Virginia.	Edmund J. Davis, of Texas.	Joseph R. Hawley, of Connecticut.	E. F. Noyes, of Ohio.
Alabama	20	12	7	1				
Arkansas	12	12						
California	12	12						
Connecticut	12	6	6					
Delaware	6		6					
Florida	8	5	3					
Georgia	22	16	6					
Illinois	42	25	17					
Indiana	30		30					
Iowa	22	19	3					
Kansas	10	10						
Kentucky	24	4	20					
Louisiana	16	5	11					
Maine	14	4	10					
Maryland	16		16					
Massachusetts	26	26						
Michigan	22		22					
Minnesota	10		10					
Mississippi	16	11	4	1				
Missouri	30	27	2				1	
Nebraska	6	2	4					
Nevada	6	6						
New Hampshire	10	10						
New Jersey	18		18					
New York	70	16	53					1
North Carolina	20	20						
Ohio	44	30	14					
Oregon	6		6					
Pennsylvania	58	58						
Rhode Island	8		8					
South Carolina	14	9	5					
Tennessee	24			24				
Texas	16					16		
Vermont	10		10					
Virginia	22				22			
West Virginia	10		10					
Wisconsin	20	15	5					
Arizona	2		2					
Colorado	2	1	1					
Dakota	2	½	1½					
District of Columbia	2		2					
Idaho	2		2					
Montana	2		2					
New Mexico	2	2						
Utah	2		2					
Washington	2		2					
Wyoming	2	1	1					
Total	752	364½	321½	26	22	16	1	1

Mr. JOHN R. POPHAM, of Virginia. *Mr. President:* Twenty delegates of Virginia desire to change their votes to that man who, in the opinion of those delegates, is by far the strongest of all others with every Republican, of whatever form, condition, or complexion; a man who is all the stronger for the reason that they respect him and reverence him for his outspoken fearlessness, his patriotism, and his integrity. I am instructed to change twenty votes to Henry Wilson and two votes for Schuyler Colfax.

Mr. STEVENSON, of West Virginia. *Mr. President:* I am instructed to change the vote of West Virginia to nine for Wilson and one for Colfax.

Mr. JOHN S. BIGBY, of Georgia. *Mr. President:* I am instructed to change the vote of Georgia so as to make it unanimous for Wilson.

The vote now stood—

Whole number	752
Necessary to a choice	377
Henry Wilson, of Massachusetts, had	399½
Schuyler Colfax, of Indiana, had	308½
Horace Maynard, of Tennessee, had	26
Edmund J. Davis, of Texas, had	16
Joseph R. Hawley, of Connecticut, had	1
Edward F. Noyes, of Ohio, had	1

At this point, although the result of the ballot had not been announced, it was apparent to all that the Hon. HENRY WILSON, of Massachusetts, had received a majority of the votes of the Convention, and the wildest demonstrations of satisfaction broke out in every part of the house. The enthusiasm was a repetition of that which was manifested when the nomination of President Grant was announced. Chairmen of delegations in different parts of the floor were, amidst all the commotion, struggling to obtain recognition by the Chair to change the votes of their States, when the floor was awarded to the chairman of the Indiana delegation.

Hon. HENRY S. LANE, of Indiana. *Mr. President:* I am instructed by the united delegation from Indiana to move that the nomination of that distinguished patriot and son of Massachusetts, Henry Wilson, be made unanimous.

The motion was put, and, the entire Convention rising *en masse*, was adopted with one swelling *aye!*

The President then announced officially the nomination of Ulysses S. Grant and Henry Wilson as candidates of the Republican party of the United States respectively for the offices of President and Vice-President in the coming election, and that the officers of the Convention would notify them officially of the choice of the Convention.

DISPATCH FROM MR. COLFAX.

The President then read the following telegraphic dispatch from Schuyler Colfax to Colonel J. W. Foster, of Indiana:

WASHINGTON, *June* 6, 1872.

JOHN W. FOSTER, *Indiana:*

Accept for yourself and delegation my sincere gratitude for your gallant contest. I support the ticket cheerfully. Men are nothing, principles everything. Nothing must arrest Republican triumph until equality under law, like liberty, from which it springs, is universally acknowledged, and the citizenship of the humblest becomes a sure protection against outrage and wrong, as was Roman citizenship of old.

SCHUYLER COLFAX.

The reading of the dispatch was received with warm applause.

THANKS OF THE CONVENTION.

Mr. CHARLES S. SPENCER, of New York, offered the following, which was applauded and adopted:

Resolved, That the thanks of this Convention are hereby heartily given to the generous citizens of Philadelphia, from whom its delegates have received the kindest treatment and the greatest courtesy.

A DELEGATE also offered a resolution of thanks to the President of the Convention for the dignity, impartiality, and ability with which he had discharged his arduous duties as presiding officer, and to the officers of the Convention; which was unanimously adopted, with cheers.

The PRESIDENT. There remains for me but one more official act to perform; which is to declare, as I now do, this Convention adjourned *sine die.*

APPENDIX.

ROLL OF DELEGATES AND ALTERNATES

TO THE

National Union Republican Convention,

HELD AT

PHILADELPHIA, JUNE 5 AND 6, 1872,

With Post Office Address of Each.

TOGETHER WITH A STATEMENT OF NUMBER OF DELEGATES TO WHICH EACH STATE WAS ENTITLED; NAMES OF OFFICERS OF THE STATE COMMITTEES, AND THE CALLS AND

PLATFORMS OF ALL THE REPUBLICAN NATIONAL CONVENTIONS

SINCE 1856.

Names and Post Office Address of Delegates and Alternates to the National Republican Convention of 1872.

[Those whose names are marked with an asterisk (*) were alternates, who attended the Convention in place of the delegates chosen.]

ALABAMA.

DELEGATES.

AT LARGE.

R. M. Reynolds..Camden, Wilcox co.
N. B. Cloud*..Montgomery, Montgomery co.
Lewis E. Parsons...Talladega, Talladega co.
P. G. Clark...Marion, Perry co.
J. W. Burke*..Jacksonville, Calhoun co.
George E. Spencer*..Decatur, Morgan co.
James P. Stowe, *Chairman*................................Montgomery.
Paul Strobach...Montgomery.

DISTRICTS—(*old apportionment.*)

1.—D. E. Coon...Selma, Dallas co.
    Philip Joseph..Mobile, Mobile co.
2.—J. V. McDuffie...Hayneville, Lowndes co.
    E. M. Kiels..Eufaula, Barbour co.
3.—Isaac Heyman...Opelika, Lee co.
    Wm. V. Turner..Wetumpka, Elmore co.
4.—W. B. Jones..Demopolis, Marengo co.
    W. G. M. Gholson.....................................Prattville, Autauga co.
5.—William Gaston*..Huntsville, Madison co.
    P. J. Smith..Attalla, Etowah co.
6.—C. C. Sheets*..Decatur, Morgan co.
    S. Bynum*..

ALTERNATES.

A. W. Jones...Evergreen, Conecuh co.
....
Wm. B. Bowen..Tuskegee, Macon co.
Joseph H. Speed...Marion, Perry co.
....
....
William Miller, Jr..Greenville, Butler co.
Alexander White...Selma, Dallas co.

James M. Jackson..Gainestown, Clarke co.
Jerre Harralson...Selma, Dallas co.
D. C. Whiting...Montgomery, Montgomery co.
B. F. Royal...Union Springs, Bullock co.
Robert S. Keffin..Wedowee, Randolph co.
Lisbon Cherry...Bluffton, Chambers co.
George M. Duskin..Greensborough, Hale co.
A. H. Curtis..Marion, Perry co.
....
J. A. De Armon..————, Calhoun co.
Thomas Oliver...Elyton, Jefferson co.
....

ARKANSAS.

AT LARGE.

Powell Clayton, *Chairman*..................Little Rock, Pulaski co..........
O. A. Hadley..................................Little Rock, Pulaski co..........
William H. Grey...............................Helena, Phillips co..........

DISTRICTS—*(old apportionment.)*

1.—Elisha Baxter..............................Batesville, Independence co..........
    Stephen Wheeler............................De Vall's Bluff, Prairie co..........
    J. H. Johnson..............................Augusta, Woodruff co..........
2.—Oliver P. Snyder..........................Pine Bluff, Jefferson co..........
    H. A. Millen...............................Camden, Ouachita co........V. V. Smith, *proxy*..........Lewisville, Lafayette co.
    Thomas V. Rankin...........................Monticello, Drew co..........
3.—J. M. Johnson.............................Huntsville, Madison co..........
    H. H. White................................Little Rock, Pulaski co..........
    E. J. Searle...............................Arkadelphia, Clark co......Geo. A. Kingston, *proxy*..........Arkadelphia, Clark co.

CALIFORNIA.

DISTRICTS.

1.—J. B. Southard*...........................San Francisco..........
    James Otis, *Chairman*.....................San Francisco..........
    James H. Withington........................San Francisco..........
2.—F. K. Shattuck............................Oakland, Alameda co..........
    J. W. B. Dickson...........................Placerville, El Dorado co..........
    H. S. Sargent..............................Stockton, San Joaquin co..........
3.—Charles M. Patterson, *Secretary*..........Marysville, Yuba co..........
    E. Wadsworth...............................Yreka, Siskiyou co..........
    A. D. Starr................................Vallejo, Solano co..........
4.—M. D. Boruck*.............................
    C. S. Abbott...............................San Juan, Monterey co..........
    Thomas Fallon..............................San José, Santa Clara co..........

CONNECTICUT.

DELEGATES.   **ALTERNATES.**

AT LARGE.

Joseph R. Hawley, *Chairman*......Hartford, Hartford co...... |
Bartlett Bent............................Middletown, Middlesex co...... |
Sabin L. Sayles.........................Killingly, Windham co...... |
John Tweedy............................Danbury, Fairfield co...... |

DISTRICTS.

1.—James D. Frary.....................New Britain, Hartford co...... |
    Lucius S. Fuller....................Tolland, Tolland co...... |
2.—Charles Parker.....................Meriden, New Haven co...... |
    Jared E. Redfield..................Essex, Middlesex co...... |
3.—Daniel Chadwick..................Lyme, New London co...... |
    George S. Moulton................Windham, Windham co...... |
4.—Joseph F. Calhoun................Torrington, Litchfield co...... |
    Israel M. Bullock..................Bridgeport, Fairfield co...... |

DELAWARE.

Henry F. Pickels........................Wilmington, New Castle co........B. S. Booth................New Castle, New Castle co.
John C. Clark............................Kirkwood, New Castle co........A. W. Lynch..............Middletown, New Castle co.
Isaac Jump................................Dover, Kent co........W. T. Collins..............Smyrna, Kent co.
James R. Lofland, *Chairman*.....Milford, Kent co........W. C. Davidson.........Milford, Kent co.
Charles F. Richards, *Secretary*....Georgetown, Sussex co........William P. Orr...........Lewes, Sussex co.
Benjamin Burton........................Georgetown, Sussex co........Simeon Pennwell......Greenwood, Sussex co.

FLORIDA.

Josiah T. Walls, *Chairman*..........Gainesville, Alachua co...... |
Dennis Eagan.............................Madison, Madison co...... |

DELEGATES AND ALTERNATES.

Frank N. Wicker..................................Key West, Monroe co........
John W. Butler...................................Milton, Santa Rosa co......
J. H. Armstrong..................................Lake City, Columbia co....
Hiram Potter, Jr.................................Pensacola, Escambia co....
James W. Johnson.................................Monticello, Jefferson co..
William H. Gleason...............................Miami, Dade co............

GEORGIA.

[*The Republican State Convention in Georgia elected thirty-three delegates to the National Convention, when under the call that State was entitled to but twenty-two; the eleven extra delegates are therefore included in this list as alternates.*]

AT LARGE.

Benjamin Conley..................................Augusta, Richmond co......Amos T. Akerman..............Cartersville, Bartow co.
Dawson A. Walker.................................Dalton, Whitfield co......Thomas J. Speer..............Milner, Pike co.
John S. Bigby, *Chairman*........................Newnan, Coweta co.........William J. White.............Augusta, Richmond co.
Moses H. Hale....................................Savannah, Chatham co......Philip Joiner................Albany, Dougherty co.
Richard H. Whiteley..............................Bainbridge, Decatur co....
John F. Quarles..................................Augusta, Richmond co......
W. B. Higginbotham...............................Rome, Floyd co............
James M. Simms...................................Savannah, Chatham co......

DISTRICTS—(*old apportionment.*)

1.—A. W. Stone...................................Savannah, Chatham co......J. T. Shufton................Brunswick, Glynn co.
    L. M. Pleasant...............................Lawton, Clinch co.........
2.—A. C. Bell...................................Preston, Webster co.......P. M. Sheibley, *Secretary*..Rome, Floyd co.
    Elbert Head..................................Americus, Sumpter co......
3.—T. M. Hogan..................................Columbus, Muscogee co.....D. C. Gresham................Greenville, Meriwether co.
    I. H. Anderson...............................Fort Valley, Houston co...
4.—George S. Fisher.............................Augusta, Richmond co......John L. Conley...............Atlanta, Fulton co.
    Jeff. F. Long................................Macon, Bibb co............

GEORGIA—Continued.

DELEGATES.	DISTRICTS—(old apportionment.)	ALTERNATES.
5.—C. H. Prince	Augusta, Richmond co	
Edwin Belcher	Augusta, Richmond co	Isham S. Fannin...............Madison, Morgan co
6.—A. T. W. Lytle	Gainesville, Hall co	Roderick D. Badger...........Atlanta, Fulton co.
Madison Davis	Athens, Clark co	
7.—George P. Burnett	Rome, Floyd co	D. D. Snyder...................Atlanta, Fulton co.
William Finch	Atlanta, Fulton co	

ILLINOIS.

AT LARGE.

Emery A. Storrs ....Chicago, Cook co.......A. McIntosh...................Wilmington, Will co.
Leonard F. Ross ....Lewiston, Fulton co......J. C. Sheldon..................Urbana, Champaign co.
Erastus N. Bates* ....Springfield, Sangamon co
George F. Dick* ....Bloomington, McLean co

DISTRICTS.

1.—J. Y. Scammon, *Chairman*.................Chicago, Cook co.......C. H. Dalton..................Thornton, Cook co.
  Louis Ellsworth......................................Naperville, DuPage co....H. D. King....................Chicago, Cook co.
2.—Herman Raster......................................Chicago, Cook co........M. Periolet....................Chicago, Cook co.
  James L. Campbell..................................Chicago, Cook co........John McArthur..............Chicago, Cook co.
3.—Clark W. Upton.....................................Waukeegan, Lake co....W. N. Brainard.............Evanston, Cook co.
  William Vocke..Chicago, Cook co.......Edward S. Taylor........Evanston, Cook co.
4.—J. H. Mayburn.......................................Elgin, Kane co...........Ralph Emerson............Rockford, Winnebago co.
  A. B. Coon ....Marengo, McHenry co.....L. O. Gillman.............Belvidere, Boone co.

DELEGATES AND ALTERNATES.

5.—John C. Smith..................Galena, Jo Daviess co......Giles F. Van Vechten..................Lanark, Carroll co.
S. S. Patterson*............——..................——..........Magnolia, Putnam co.
6.—Andrew Crawford..............Genesee, Henry co........D. B. Fife..................——
J. W. Templeton................Princeton, Bureau co......C. Lynde, Jr..................Rock Island, Rock Island co.
7.—Lyman B. Ray..................Morris, Grundy co........George W. Lane..................Morris, Grundy co.
Warren M. Sweetland ....Newark, Kendall co......Colguhan Grant..................Morris, Grundy co.
8.—Warren R. Hickox ....Kankakee, Kankakee co..Winfield S. Campbell..................Manteno, Kankakee co.
N. S. Stevens..................Paxton, Ford co..........J. R. Parsons..................——, Livingston co.
9.—Enoch Emery..................Peoria, Peoria co........William J. Phelps..................Elmwood, Peoria co.
George V. Deitrich*..............Galesburg, Knox co......——..................——
10.—John McKinney, Sr.............Oquawka, Henderson co....Thomas Logan..................——, Hancock co.
Henry Tubbs...................Young America, Warren co..E. K. Westfall..................——, McDonough co.
11.—George W. Burns..............Quincy, Adams co........Joseph B. Gilpin..................Quincy, Adams co.
David Pierson..................Carrollton, Greene co....George W. Ware..................Jerseyville, Jersey co.
12.—Shelby M. Cullom..............Springfield, Sangamon co..A. C. Vandewater..................Pana, Christian co.
John Moses...................Winchester, Scott co......J. C. Conkling..................Springfield, Sangamon co.
13.—Frank Hoblett*................——, Logan co............——..................——
Thomas Snell.................Clinton, DeWitt co........Jacob Copples..................——, Mason co.
14.—Joseph R. Mosser..............Decatur, Macon co........Wood M. Townsend..................Danville, Vermillion co.
James Knight.................Danville, Vermillion co....M. L. Dunlap..................Champaign City, Champaign co.
15.—Thomas A. Apperson............Ætna, Cumberland co......Samuel W. Moulton..................Shelbyville, Shelby co.
James Steele..................Paris, Edgar co..........Thomas A. Stewart..................——, Lawrence co.
16.—Henry C. Goodnow..............Salem, Marion co........John Cunningham..................——, Marion co.
J. F. Alexander................Greenville, Bond co......Joseph T. Eccles..................Hillsboro', Montgomery co.
17.—Russell Hinckley...............Bellville, St. Clair co....John Thomas..................Bellville, St. Clair co.
A. W. Metcalf................Edwardsville, Madison co..Henry M. Kimball..................Carlinville, Macoupin co.
18.—Robert Harmer*...............——..................D. L. Davis..................——, Alexander co.
Thomas H. Burgess..............Duquoin, Perry co........D. R. McMasters..................——, Randolph co.
19.—Geo. R. Edwards*..............——..................Amos B. Barrett..................Mt. Vernon, Jefferson co.
Israel A. Powell................Olney, Richland co......David W. Barclay..................Fairfield, Wayne co.

INDIANA.

DELEGATES.

AT LARGE.

Henry S. Lane, *Chairman*	Crawfordsville, Montgomery co.	C. W. Cathcart...... La Porte, La Porte co.
Richard W. Thompson*		H. C. Newcomb...... Indianapolis, Marion co.
George K. Steele	Rockville, Parke co.	Thomas C. Jacques...... Poseyville, Posey co.
T. C. Slaughter	Corydon, Harrison co.	Ira G. Grover...... Greensburg, Decatur co.
C. W. Chapman	Warsaw, Kosciusko co.	John Beard...... Crawfordsville, Montgomery co.
Sol. Meredith	Cambridge City, Wayne co.	W. W. Carter...... Bowling Green, Clay co.
Robert McCary	Indianapolis.	
W. H. Russell*		

DISTRICTS.

1.—James C. Denny	Vincennes, Knox co.	Roan Clark...... Rome, Perry co.
Levi Ferguson	Petersburg, Pike co.	J. W. Burton...... Washington, Daviess co.
2.—Jesse J. Brown	New Albany, Floyd co.	J. H. McCampbell...... Jeffersonville, Clark co.
W. S. Ferrier	Charlestown, Clark co.	R. M. Wellman...... Jasper, Dubois co.
3.—Joseph I. Irwin	Columbus, Bartholomew co.	R. L. Davis...... Rising Sun, Ohio co.
H. C. Vincent	Gilford, Dearborn co.	Thomas C. Batchelor...... Vernon, Jennings co.
4.—J. C. McIntosh	Connersville, Fayette co.	D. M. Stewart...... Rushville, Rush co.
C. C. Binkley	Richmond, Wayne co.	W. R. Hough...... Greenfield, Hancock co.
5.—D. E. Williamson	Greencastle, Putnam co.	
W. C. Sandefur	Franklin, Johnson co.	
6.—Chas. Cruft	Terre Haute, Vigo co.	W. W. Carter...... Bowling Green, Clay co.
J. B. Mulky	Bloomington, Monroe co.	Wm. A. Montgomery...... Gosport, Owen co.
7.—John H. Gould	Delphi, Carroll co.	David B. Carter...... Frankfort, Clinton co.
George Nebeker	Covington, Fountain co.	Thomas Underwood...... La Fayette, Tippecanoe co.
8.—Thomas Jay	Kokomo, Howard co.	M. F. Tingley...... Marion, Grant co.
M. S. Robinson	Anderson, Madison co.	G. I. Reed...... Peru, Miami co.
9.—M. L. Bundy	Newcastle Henry co.	J. J. Todd...... Bluffton, Wells co.
George A. Dent	Decatur, Adams co.	John W. Heddington...... Portland, Jay co.

DELEGATES AND ALTERNATES.   9

10.—Frank Macartney............................Angola, Steuben co.......C. O. Myers................................Kendallville, Noble co.
    W. H. Trammel.............................Huntington, Huntington co.......R. Wes. McBride............................Waterloo, DeKalb co.
11.—William G. George.........................South Bend, St. Joseph co.......M. L. McClelland..........................Valparaiso, Porter co.
    E. P. Hammond............................Rensselaer, Jasper co.......L. C. Rose................................La Porte, La Porte co.

IOWA.
AT LARGE.

Grenville M. Dodge, *Ch'rman*..Council Bluffs, Pottawattomie co........J. S. Hurley................................Wapello, Louisa co.
W. H. Seevers.................................Oskaloosa, Mahaska co........J. E. Burke................................Waverly, Bremer co.
I. W. Card....................................Mason City, Cerro Gordo co........John Bersheim..............................Council Bluffs.
Alexander Clark...............................Muscatine, Muscatine co........J. W. Havens...............................Sigourney, Keokuk co.

DISTRICTS—(*old apportionment.*)

1.—C. W. Slagle...............................Fairfield, Jefferson co........
   Samuel M. Clark............................Keokuk, Lee co........E. W. Tatlock..............................Wapello, Louisa co.
   Norman Everson.............................Washington, Washington co........J. M. Shaffer..............................Fairfield, Jefferson co.
2.—John W. Green..............................Davenport, Scott co........E. S. Bailey...............................Clinton, Clinton co.
   Sylvanus Yates.............................Tipton, Cedar co........John McKean................................Anamosa, Jones co.
   S. L. Baker................................Andrew, Jackson co........J. S. McClure..............................Fairfax, Linn co.
3.—William Vandever..........................Dubuque, Dubuque co........E. S. Fonda................................Osage, Mitchell co.
   Andy J. Felt...............................Nashua, Chickasaw co........Danford Eddy...............................Luana, Clayton co.
   John H. Gear*..............................Burlington, Des Moines co........H. C. Bulis................................Decorah, Winneshiek co.
4.—H. S. Winslow..............................Newton, Jasper co........S. T. Caldwell.............................Eddyville, Wapello co.
   F. M. Drake................................Centerville, Appanoose co........N. B. Vineyard.............................Marengo, Iowa co.
   H. G. Little...............................Grinnell, Poweshiek co........A. B. Cornell..............................Iowa City, Johnson co.
5.—A. R. Anderson............................Sidney, Fremont co........D. F. Sellards.............................Mount Ayr, Ringgold co.
   W. S. Dungan...............................Chariton, Lucas co........B. F. Murray...............................Winterset, Madison co.
   J. S. McIntyre.............................Clarinda, Page co........Lewis Todhunter............................Indianola, Warren co.
6.—Isaac Pendleton...........................Sioux City, Woodbury co........A. C. Call.................................Algona, Kossuth co.
   P. H. Conger...............................Waterloo, Blackhawk co........D. Carr Early..............................Sac City, Sac co.
   J. L. Williams.............................Marshalltown, Marshall co........J. M. Berry................................Webster City, Hamilton co.

KANSAS.

DELEGATES.

Name	Location	Alternate	Location
Benjamin F. Simpson, *Chairman*	Paola, Miami co.	R. E. Stephenson	Olathe, Johnson co.
Henry Buckingham	Concordia, Cloud co.	A. A. Thomas	Cawker City, Mitchell co.
John A. Martin	Atchison, Atchison co.	Frederick Close	Highland, Doniphan co.
H. C. Cross	Emporia, Lyon co.	E. S. Nichols	Garnett, Anderson co.
George Noble, *Secretary*	Lawrence, Douglas co.	M. S. Thomson	Wyandotte, Wyandotte co.
Josiah Kellogg	Leavenworth, Leavenworth co.	S. F. Eggers	Oskaloosa, Jefferson co.
Charles A. Morris	Fort Scott, Bourbon co.	Percy Daniels	Girard, Crawford co.
William Baldwin	Witchita, Sedgwick co.	J. V. Fairbanks	Winfield, Cowley co.
Thomas Newton*	Leavenworth, Leavenworth co.		
John C. Carpenter	New Chicago, Neosho co.	S. J. Smith	Independence, Montgomery co.

KENTUCKY.

AT LARGE.

Name	Location	Alternate	Location
James Speed	Louisville, Jefferson co.	Geo. H. Griffith	Louisville, Jefferson co.
William Cassius Goodloe, *Chairman*	Lexington, Fayette co.	John F. Thomas	Paducah, McCracken co.
Walter Evans	Hopkinsville, Christian co.	S. Casey	Caseyville, Union co.
John G. Eve	Barboursville, Knox co.		
Peter Smith*	Frankfort, Franklin co.		
R. M. Kelly	Louisville, Jefferson co.		

DISTRICTS—(*old apportionment.*)

Name	Location	Alternate	Location
1.—Geo. H. Dobyns*	Lancaster, Garrard co.	W. Waller	Benton, Marshall co.
Samuel L. Casey	Caseyville, Union co.	John F. Thomas	Paducah, McCracken co.
2.—John B. Bruner	Hardinsburg, Breckinridge co.	Thos. Randall	Madisonville, Hopkins co.
Eli H. Murray	Louisville, Jefferson co.	Malcom McIntire	Hartford, Ohio co.
3.—W. B. Craddock	Munfordville, Hart co.	F. H. Richardson	Bowling Green, Warren co.
R. A. Green	Bowling Green, Warren co.	J. P. Coleman	Bowling Green, Warren co.

DELEGATES AND ALTERNATES.   11

4.—W. H. Hays*..................................Springfield, Washington co.......|...Elizabethtown, Hardin co.
   T. E. Burns, *Secretary*..............Lebanon, Marion co......A. H. Churchill...............|
5.—Lewis Buckner............................Louisville, Jefferson co.......Thos. G. Griffith............Louisville, Jefferson co.
   W. H. Gibson................................Louisville, Jefferson co.......|
6.—J. W. Robbins.............................Falmouth, Pendleton co.......Henry Myers................Covington, Kenton co.
   Ben. P. Gray*...............................New Castle, Henry co.......E. W. Hawkins...........Newport, Campbell co.
7.—A. H. Adams...............................Lexington, Fayette co.......G. J. Doran....................Danville, Boyle co.
   William R. Fleming....................Lexington, Fayette co.......T. R. Jackson...................Lexington, Fayette co.
8.—J. W. Caperton...........................Richmond, Madison co........|
   William Berkle*..........................Bryantsville, Garrard co......|
9.—Thos. A. Davis...........................Maysville, Mason co.......W. W. Culbertson...........Catlettsburg, Boyd co.
   John Means..................................Ashland, Boyd co......James Howard..................Mt. Sterling, Montgomery co.

LOUISIANA.

AT LARGE.

Jas. Lewis, *Chairman*................................New Orleans.......P. B. S. Pinchback............New Orleans.
Louis Trager...............................Black Hawk Point, Concordia Parish......E. Joubert.........................New Orleans.
E. C. Billings...New Orleans.......B. J. Kennedy......................New Orleans.
John Ray......................................Monroe, Ouachita Parish.......O. C. Blandin....................New Orleans.
George W. Carter......................................New Orleans.......|
G. Casanave..New Orleans.......|

DISTRICTS.

1.—Jas. B. Wands...........................Amite City, Tangipahoa Parish.....E. E. Norton....................New Orleans.
   C. J. Adolph...New Orleans.......P. Leonard.........St. Sophie P. O., Plaquemines Parish.
2.—W. G. Elliott..New Orleans.......T. B. Stamps............Carrollton, Jefferson Parish.
   Mortimer F. Smith, Edgard P.O., St. John the Baptist Parish......A. Jay Smith....................New Orleans.
3.—C. B. Darrall..........................Brashear City, St. Mary's Parish.....G. H. Hill.............Donaldsonville, Ascension Parish.
   J. Henri Burch......Baton Rouge, East Baton Rouge Parish.....Geo. Williams..........Baton Rouge, East Baton Rouge Parish.

LOUISIANA—Continued.

	DELEGATES.	DISTRICTS.	ALTERNATES.
4.—	E. L. Weber............St. Francisville, West Feliciana Parish........	J. H. Hall........	
	Harry Lott........................Alexandria, Rapides Parish........	J. H. McVea........	
5.—	E. W. Robinson............Waterproof P. O., Tensas Parish........	————	
	W. F. Southard*................Monroe, Ouachita Parish........	————	

MAINE.

AT LARGE.

Isaiah Stetson, *Chairman*............Bangor, Penobscot co......	John Hall............	........South Berwick, York co.
Seth Tisdale*..........................Ellsworth, Hancock co......	Seth E. Bryant........	
Frederick Robie..................Gorham, Cumberland co......	Edmund Flye..........	......New Castle, Lincoln co.
Enoch C. Farrington..........Fryeburgh, Oxford co......	Fred. C. Perkins......	......Farmington, Franklin co.

DISTRICTS.

1.—Stanley T. Pullen............Portland, Cumberland co......	Luther Billings........	......Bridgton, Cumberland co.
John E. Butler........................Biddeford, York co......	Seth E. Bryant........	
2.—Frederic E. Shaw........................Paris, Oxford co......	William A. Bradley....	......Fryeburgh, Oxford co.
Alexander H. S. Davis..........Farmington, Franklin co......	Seward Dill............	......Phillips, Franklin co.
3.—Hiram Bliss, Jr..............................Washington, Knox co......	————	
Joseph F. Sanborn*................Readfield, Kennebec co......	Arnold S. Richmond....	......Monmouth, Kennebec co.
4.—Sylvanus H. Hussey............Houlton, Aroostook co......	Russell Kittredge......	......Dover, Piscataquis co.
Ezra C. Brett....................Bangor, Penobscot co......	Charles A. Boutelle....	......Bangor, Penobscot co.
5.—Albert G. Jewett..................Belfast, Waldo co......	John S. Case..........	......Rockland, Knox co.
Joseph T. Grant..................Ellsworth, Hancock co......	Parker Tuck..........	......Bucksport, Hancock co.

MARYLAND.

AT LARGE.

Jacob Tome.................................Port Deposit, Cecil co.
Thomas A. Spence.....................Princess Ann, Somerset co.
Daniel Weisel.............................Hagerstown, Washington co.
Charles C. Fulton......................Baltimore city.

DISTRICTS.

1.—William H. Barton..........Cambridge, Dorchester co.......William H. H. Farrow.......Snow Hill, Worcester co.
　　William Perkins................Chestertown, Kent co............Samuel T. Hopkins............Easton, Talbot co.
2.—John T. Ensor..................Towsontown, Baltimore co.....A. M. Hancock..................Creswell, Harford co.
　　William L. W. Seabrook....Westminster, Carroll co.........D. K. Ralston....................Port Deposit, Cecil co.
3.—Robert Turner...................Baltimore city......................Jacob Seaton....................Baltimore city.
　　Thomas Kelso....................Baltimore city......................Augustus Roberts..............Baltimore city.
4.—Samuel M. Shoemaker.....Baltimore city......................Walter Sorrell...................Baltimore city.
　　John M. McClintock..........Baltimore city......................Samuel W. Chase..............Baltimore city.
5.—James A. Gary, *Chairman*..Annapolis, Anne Arundel co...W. G. Tuck, *Secretary*......Annapolis, Anne Arundel co.
　　Alexander Randall............Annapolis, Anne Arundel co....A. A. Lawrence................Leonardtown, St. Mary's co.
6.—Hopewell Hebb.................Cumberland, Allegany co......A. R. Appleman...............Hagerstown, Washington co.
　　John L. Linthicum............Middletown, Frederick co.....Henry C. England............Rockville, Montgomery co.

MASSACHUSETTS.

AT LARGE.

Alexander H. Rice...................................Boston........Edward W. Kinsley...................Boston.
George B. Loring, *Chairman*..................Salem..........Charles E. Whiting................Northbridge.
P. Emory Aldrich....................................Worcester....Amasa Norcross....................Fitchburg.
William Claflin.......................................Newton.......Thomas Talbot......................North Billerica.
Oliver Ames..Easton........Cyrus Wakefield...................Wakefield.
Sylvander Johnson..................................North Adams.....Henry S. Briggs.................Pittsfield.

MASSACHUSETTS—Continued.

DELEGATES.	DISTRICTS—(old apportionment.)	ALTERNATES.
1.—Jonathan Bourne, Jr..............	New Bedford........	John S. Brayton................Fall River.
John B. D. Coggswell.................	Yarmouth............	William T. Davis.................Plymouth.
2.—Seth Turner..............................	Randolph............	Hawkes Fearing, Jr.............Hingham.
C. C. Bixby.................................	No. Bridgewater...	J. S. Anthony......................Taunton.
3.—Robert K. Potter*....................	Boston................	————————................Boston.
Solomon B. Stebbins.................	Boston................	W. W. Doherty.....................Boston.
4.—Joshua B. Smith.......................	Cambridge...........	J. Otis Wetherbee.................Boston.
Richard Beeching.......................	East Boston..........	John J. Smith.......................Boston.
5.—Edwin Patch*...........................	Lynn....................	————————................————.
John F. Harris.............................	Marblehead..........	Richard Couch...............Newburyport.
6.—Eugene L. Norton.....................	Charlestown.........	Daniel Allen.....................Wakefield.
William E. Blunt.........................	Haverhill..............	Jacob Emerson.....................Methuen.
7.—Joshua N. Marshall..................	Lowell.................	J. A. Harwood.....................Littleton.
Edwin C. Morse..........................	Natick..................	George K. Daniel................Needham.
8.—E. B. Stoddard.........................	Worcester............	George C. Brigham............Westboro.
Daniel W. Taft............................	Uxbridge..............	F. D. Brown.........................Webster.
9.—Otis T. Ruggles.......................	Fitchburg.............	Elisha Brimhall...................Clinton.
Horatio G. Knight.......................	East Hampton......	William B. Hale............Northampton.
10.—Henry J. Bush.........................	Westfield.............	L. H. Taylor....................Springfield.
H. H. Richardson........................	Pittsfield..............	John Branning..........................Lee.

MICHIGAN.

AT LARGE.

E. B. Ward..Detroit, Wayne co........F. C. Beaman................Adrian, Lenawee co.
George Williard................................Battle Creek, Calhoun co........H. G. Wells................Kalamazoo, Kalamazoo co.
Wm. A. Howard, *Chairman*............Grand Rapids, Kent co........Alonzo Sessions................Ionia, Ionia co.
Perry Hannah....................Traverse City, Grand Traverse co........J. G. Ramsdell................Grand Haven, Ottowa co.

DELEGATES AND ALTERNATES. 15

DISTRICTS.

1.—Newell Avery..................Detroit, Wayne co........E. W. Meddaugh..................Detroit, Wayne co.
   John Greusel..................Detroit, Wayne co........John Gibson....................Detroit, Wayne co.
2.—Nathan N. Kendall.............Monroe, Monroe co........Lucius Lilley..................Tecumseh, Lenawee co.
   R. A. Beal....................Ann Arbor, Washtenaw co..H. D. Farnham..................Hillsdale, Hillsdale co.
3.—Harvey Bush...................Jackson, Jackson co......D. R. Cooley...................Union City, Branch co.
   J. C. Fitzgerald..............Marshall, Calhoun co.....E. S. Lacey....................Charlotte, Eaton co.
4.—George S. Clapp...............St. Joseph, Berrien co...C. A. Harrison.................Paw Paw, Van Buren co.
   James H. Stone................Kalamazoo, Kalamazoo co..J. G. Wait.....................Sturgis, St. Joseph co.
5.—B. D. Pritchard...............Allegan, Allegan co......J. W. Stone....................Allegan, Allegan co.
   H. A. Norton..................Berlin, Ottawa co........M. B. Beers....................Ionia, Ionia co.
6.—J. W. Begole..................Flint, Genesee co........Fred. J. Lee...................Howell, Livingston co.
   D. L. Crossman................Williamston, Ingham co...C. F. Kimball..................Pontiac, Oakland co.
7.—Ezra Hazen....................Memphis, St. Clair co....E. F. Mead.....................Romeo, Macomb co.
   B. W. Huston..................Vassar, Tuscola co.......John Divine....................Lexington, Sanilac co.
8.—C. S. Draper..................East Saginaw, Saginaw co.W. R. Burt.....................East Saginaw, Saginaw co.
   James Birney..................Bay City, Bay co.........N. B. Bradley..................Bay City, Bay co.
9.—B. F. Rogers..................Ontonagon, Ontonagon co..W. L. Wetmore..................Marquette, Marquette co.
   J. F. Brown...................Big Rapids, Mecosta co...D. L. Benton...................Big Rapids, Mecosta co.

MINNESOTA.

AT LARGE.

C. T. Benedict..................Rochester, Olmsted co......G. B. Cooley..................Mantorville, Dodge co.
A. E. Rice......................Wilmar, Kandiyohi co......Asa B. Hutchinson.............Hutchinson, McLeod co.
D. M. Sabin, *Chairman*.........Stillwater, Washington co.H. B. Prince..................Stillwater, Washington co.
Otto Wallmark...................Chisago City, Chisago co..Oscar Ross....................Taylor's Falls, Chisago co.

DISTRICTS.

1.—J. T. Williams................Mankato, Blue Earth co....W. D. Rice....................St. James, Watonwan co.
   A. C. Dodge, *Secretary*......Owatonna Steel co.........A. C. Woolfolk................Mankato, Blue Earth co.

MINNESOTA—Continued.

DELEGATES.		ALTERNATES.
2.—R. F. Crowell*	St. Paul, Ramsey co.	William Bickell............St. Peter, Nicollet co.
C. H. Goodsell*	Northfield, Rice co.	
3.—W. E. Hicks	Alexandria, Douglass co.	
William S. King	Minneapolis, Hennepin co.	I. C. Walters............Brainard, Crow Wing co.

MISSISSIPPI.

AT LARGE.

O. C. French, *Secretary*............Natchez, Adams co............M. Howard............Fayette, Jefferson co.
A. Warner............Canton, Madison co............G. W. Wells............Holly Springs, Marshall co.
B. K. Bruce............Beulah, Bolivar co............B. A. Lee............Vicksburg, Warren co.
A. T. Morgan............Yazoo, Yazoo co............A. Henderson............Palo Alto, Chickasaw co.

DISTRICTS.

1.—R. W. Flourney............Pontotoc, Pontotoc co.
L. J. Seurlock............Water Valley, Yallabusha co.
2.—B. Harrington............Friar's Point, Coahoma co............L. C. Abbott............Holly Springs, Marshall co.
James Hill............Holly Springs, Marshall co............J. H. Johnson............Hernando, De Soto co.
3.—F. M. Abbott............West Point, Colfax co............H. C. Powers............Starkville, Oktibbeha co.
A. K. Davis............Macon, Noxubee co............J. W. Chandler............Macon, Noxubee co.
4.—J. H. Sumner............Lexington, Holmes co............J. J. Spellman............Canton, Madison co.
William Breck............Canton, Madison co............W. W. Chisholm............DeKalb, Kemper co.
5.—Edwin Hill............Vicksburg, Warren co.
James Lynch, *Chairman*............Jackson, Hinds co.
6.—J. R. Lynch............Natchez, Adams co.
A. Parker............Liberty, Amite co.

DELEGATES AND ALTERNATES. 17

MISSOURI.

AT LARGE.

John B. Henderson..................St. Louis.......S. S. Burdett..................Osceola, St. Clair co.
John F. Benjamin..................Shelbina, Shelby co......P. L. Kelley..................Mt. Vernon, Lawrence co.
George B. Wedley..................St. Louis......Moses Dixon..................Kansas City.

DISTRICTS—(old apportionment.)

1.—Chauncey I. Filley..................St. Louis......J. H. Johnson..................St. Louis.
Henry A. Clover..................St. Louis......William Kreiter..................St. Louis.
John C. Orrick..................St. Louis......Otto C. Ladermann..................St. Louis.
2.—Gustavus A. Finkelnburg..................St. Louis......E. W. Bishop..................Rolla, Phelps co.
Henry T. Blow, *Chairman*..................St. Louis......John S. Cavender..................St. Louis.
E. O. Stanard..................St. Louis......D. Q. Gale..................Washington, Franklin co.
3.—George A. Moser..................Ironton, Iron co......A. H. Adams..................Cape Girardeau, Cape Girardeau co.
Gustave St. Gem..................St. Genevieve, St. Genevieve co......G. I. Van Allen..................Potosi, Washington co.
B. B. Cahoon..................Fredericktown, Madison co......William T. Stepp..................Salem, Linn co.
4.—W. F. Cloud..................Carthage, Jasper co......W. E. Conner..................Stockton, Cedar co.
J. M. Filler..................Mt. Vernon, Lawrence co......J. N. Moore..................Long's Mill, Stone co.
J. P. Ellis..................Springfield, Greene co......A. F. Lewis..................Lebanon, Laclede co.
5.—John H. Stover..................Versailles, Morgan co......W. J. Terrell..................
M. McMillan..................Boonville, Cooper co......H. B. Johnson..................Jefferson City, Cole co.
W. Q. Dallmeyer..................Jefferson City, Cole co......George R. Smith..................Sedalia, Pettis co.
6.—William Warner..................Kansas City, Jackson co......M. L. Demotte..................Lexington, La Fayette co.
R. T. Van Horn..................Kansas City, Jackson co......M. L. Laughlin..................Marshall, Saline co.
J. J. Heizel...M. A. Lowe..................Hamilton, Caldwell co.
7.—P. A. Thompson..................Phelps City, Atchison co......A. H. Vandevert..................Gallatin, Davis co.
N. A. Winters..................Trenton, Grundy co......J. J. Clark..................
John L. Bittinger..................St. Joseph, Buchanan co......B. F. Marshall..................St. Joseph, Buchanan co.

MISSOURI—Continued.

DELEGATES.	DISTRICTS.	ALTERNATES.
8.—A. F. Denny	Huntsville, Randolph co......I. V. Pratt	Linneus, Linn co.
J. R. Peters	Memphis, Scotland co......J. R. Winchell	Hannibal, Marion co.
William Bishop	Clark City, Clark co......J. M. London	Macon City, Macon co.
9.—Edwin Draper	Louisiana, Pike co......C. W. Selfridge	————
D. P. Dyer	Louisiana, Pike co......G. R. Reich	St. Charles, St. Charles co.
Theodore Bruere	St. Charles, St. Charles co......E. Kenpinsky	Warrenton, Warren co.

NEBRASKA.

John I. Redick, *Chairman*	Omaha, Douglas co......Joseph Fox	Omaha, Douglas co.
John Roberts	Nebraska City, Otoe co......Isaac Wills	————, Cass co.
John S. Bowen	Blair, Washington co......A. H. Bowen	————, Adams co.
J. B. Weston	Beatrice, Gage co......W. F. Chapin	Lincoln, Lancaster co.
John D. Neligh	West Point, Cuming co......G. W. Dorsey	Fremont, Dodge co.
Henry M. Atkinson	Brownville, Nemaha co......T. P. Kennard	Lincoln, Lancaster co.

NEVADA.

L. H. Head	Ruby Valley, Elko co......T. H. McGrath	Virginia City, Storey co.
George M. Sabin	Pioche, Lincoln co......W. B. Morse	Hamilton, White Pine co.
John G. Grier	Silver City, Lyon co......R. L. Horton	Austin, Lander co.
J. W. Haines	Genoa, Douglass co......J. D. Minor	Carson City, Ormsby co.
C. H. Eastman	Reno, Washoe co......Wm. L. Flagler	Belmont, Nye co.
C. C. Stevenson, *Chairman*	Virginia City, Storey co......J. G. McClinton	Aurora, Esmeralda co.

NEW HAMPSHIRE.

AT LARGE.

William H. Y. Hackett................................Portsmouth.......George W. Marston...............................Portsmouth.
Frederick Smyth, *Chairman*....................Manchester.......Samuel Upton....................................Manchester.
James W. Johnson....................................Enfield...........Samuel D. Quarles...............................Ossipee.
Ossian Ray..Lancaster.......Charles W. Rand.................................Littleton.

DISTRICTS.

1.—Charles S. Whitehouse........................Rochester........Samuel G. Fisher.................................Dover.
     Albert G. Folsom................................Laconia..........Martin A. Haynes................................Gilford.
2.—Oren C. Moore, *Secretary*....................Nashua..........Nathan P. Kidder................................Manchester.
     Daniel Barnard..................................Franklin..........A. M. Stuart.....................................Franklin.
3.—Dexter Richards.................................Newport.........E. H. Cheney....................................Lebanon.
     George B. Twitchell............................Keene...........Edmund Brown..................................Lancaster.

NEW JERSEY.

AT LARGE.

Cortlandt Parker, *Chairman*.....................Newark, Essex co.......John S. Irick...........................Vincentown, Burlington co.
Alexander G. Cattell................................Merchantville, Camden co.......Jonathan Dixon...................Jersey City.
Levi D. Jarrard.......................................New Brunswick, Middlesex co.......A. S. Livingston.................Trenton, Mercer co.
J. Wyman Jones....................................Englewood, Bergen co.......Joseph Coult.....................Newton, Sussex co.

DISTRICTS.

1.—John W. Newlin.................................Millville, Cumberland co.......Coleman F. Leaming...............Cape May, Cape May co.
     Augustus S. Barber............................Woodbury, Gloucester co.......B. F. Archer.
2.—Charles Hewitt..................................Trenton, Mercer co.......William Moon......................May's Landing, Atlantic co.
     Isaac W. Carmichael..........................Ton's River, Ocean co.......James Buchanan....................Trenton, Mercer co.
3.—Amos Clark, Jr..................................Elizabeth, Union co.......P. Cortelyou.......................Mattewan, Monmouth co.
     John W. Herbert.................................Marlborough, Monmouth co.......John N. Edgar......................Summit, Union co.

NEW JERSEY—Continued.

DELEGATES. DISTRICTS. ALTERNATES.

4.—David Vickers..............Deckertown, Sussex co........Hugh M. Gaston.................Somerville, Somerset co.
F. A. Potts...................Pittstown, Hunterdon co......Samuel S. Clark..............Belvidere, Warren co.
5.—George Wurts...............Paterson, Passaic co.........Adam Carr....................Paterson, Passaic co.
Columbus Beach*..............Rockaway, Morris co..........—
6.—Frederick H. Harris........Newark, Essex co............D. W. Baker..................Newark, Essex co.
Daniel Dodd..................Newark, Essex co............A. P. Condit.................Orange, Essex co.
7.—James Gopsill..............Jersey City.................J. M. Cornelison.............Jersey City.
D. S. Gregory................Jersey City.................B. F. Hart...................Hoboken, Hudson co.

NEW YORK.

AT LARGE.

Gerrit Smith.................Peterboro, Madison co.......Andrew D. White..............Ithaca, Tompkins co.
William Orton................New York city...............William J. Bacon.............Utica, Onieda co.
James N. Matthews............Buffalo, Erie co............Freeman Clarke...............Rochester, Monroe co.
William F. Butler............New York city...............James W. Booth...............New York city.
Horace B. Claflin............Brooklyn....................John C. Robinson.............Binghamton, Broome co.
Stephen B. Moffitt...........Plattsburgh, St. Lawrence co..John A. Griswold............Troy, Rensselaer co.

DISTRICTS.

1.—John A. King...............Great Neck, Queens co.......Morgan Morgans...............Cutchogue, Suffolk co.
Stephen B. French............Sag Harbor, Suffolk co......D. H. Cortelyou..............Richmond, Richmond co.
2.—Henry C. Bowen.............Brooklyn....................George Thomas................Brooklyn.
Nelson Shaurman..............Brooklyn....................Lorin Palmer.................Brooklyn.
3.—Stewart L. Woodford........Brooklyn....................Frederick Cocheu.............Brooklyn.
Abram B. Baylis..............Brooklyn....................Albert Ammerman..............Brooklyn.
4.—Charles Jones..............Brooklyn....................Mathias J. Petre.............Brooklyn.
David Williams...............Brooklyn....................John Davies..................Brooklyn.

DELEGATES AND ALTERNATES. 21

- 5.—Henry A. Hurlbut..........................New York city......Pierre C. Van Wyck..................New York city.
- James Winterbottom........................New York city......Henry V. Crawford..................New York city.
- 6.—William Laimbeer..........................New York city......Henry Theobold.....................New York city.
- William E. Dodge............................New York city......H. E. Crampton....................New York city.
- 7.—Augustus Weismann........................New York city......Solon B. Smith....................New York city.
- Jacob M. Patterson, Jr....................New York city......C. D. Van Wagenen.................New York city.
- 8.—Charles S. Spencer........................New York city......John H. White.....................New York city.
- John D. Lawson..............................New York city......James W. Farr.....................New York city.
- 9.—H. D. Lapaugh.................................New York city......J. Schoenhoff.....................New York city.
- Joel W. Mason.................................New York city......Joseph Cudlipp....................New York city.
- 10.—William Haw, Jr............................New York city......William A. Wheelock...............New York city.
- Salem H. Wales................................New York city......Louis Naumann.....................New York city.
- 11.—D. Ogden Bradley........Dobbs' Ferry, Westchester co......Seth B. Coles............Nyack, Rockland co.
- David Robinson............Cold Spring, Putnam co......Robert R. Morris....Westchester, Westchester co.
- 12.—Ambrose S. Murray..............Goshen, Orange co......Cyrus B. Martin..........Newburgh, Orange co.
- Clinton V. R. Luddington......Monticello, Sullivan co......Gideon Wales............Pike Pond, Sullivan co.
- 13.—B. Platt Carpenter......Poughkeepsie, Dutchess co......Lemuel Sisson........Mabbettsville, Dutchess co.
- Lewis F. Payne..........Chatham Village, Columbia co......Nelson P. Aiken........Philmont, Columbia co.
- 14.—William S. Kenyon............Kingston, Ulster co......Joseph M. Boies...........Saugerties, Ulster co.
- Samuel Harris...................Catskill, Greene co......Thaddeus Hait..............Modena, Ulster co.
- 15.—Charles H. Adams..............Cohoes, Albany co......Charles P. Easton.........Albany, Albany co.
- Henry Smith.....................Albany, Albany co......Charles C. Kromer.......Schoharie, Schoharie co.
- 16.—Martin I. Townsend, *Chairman*......Troy, Rensselaer co......William H. Tefft......Whitehall, Washington co.
- James Harper..............Cambridge, Washington co.
- 17.—John Hammond............Crown Point, Essex co......John H. Whiteside........Champlain, Clinton co.
- N. Edson Sheldon........Glen's Falls, Warren co......Robert Waddell..........Wevertown, Warren co.
- 18.—William Andrus............Malone, Franklin co......Howard M. King...........Malone, Franklin co.
- Edward W. Foster......Potsdam, St. Lawrence co......George M. Gleason......Gouverneur, St. Lawrence co.
- 19.—Richard Franchot......Schenectady, Schenectady co......D. V. Berry........Fonda, Montgomery co.
- Charles S. Lester......Saratoga Springs, Saratoga co......David A. Wells........Gloversville, Fulton co.

NEW YORK—Continued.

DELEGATES.	DISTRICTS.	ALTERNATES.
20.—Leroy E. Bowe............................Otego, Otsego co.	William H. Ruggles....................Cooperstown, Otsego co.
Robert Barnard..........................Greene, Chenango co.	B. Gage Berry............................Norwich, Chenango co.
21.—Warner Miller........................Herkimer, Herkimer co.	John C. Wright..........................Copenhagen, Lewis co.
Alexander Campbell..................Watertown, Jefferson co.	H. S. Hendee.............................Carthage, Jefferson co.
22.—Daniel Walker........................North Gage, Oneida co.	C. P. Hayes...............................Forestport, Oneida co.
M. D. Barnett.............................Rome, Oneida co.	A. J. Coggeshall.........................Waterville, Oneida co.
23.—Andrew S. Warner.....................Pulaski, Oswego co.	De Witt Gardner........................Fulton, Oswego co.
Alexander M. Holmes..............Morrisville, Madison co.	William H. Brand....................Leonardsville, Madison co.
24.—R. Nelson Gere....................Syracuse, Onondaga co.	Abram P. Smith........................Cortlandville, Cortland co.
David Allen Munro................Camillus, Onondaga co.	Carroll E. Smith........................Syracuse, Onondaga co.
25.—George I. Post......................Fairhaven, Cayuga co.	T. (t. Yeomans.........................Walworth, Wayne co.
George W. Jones........................Ovid, Seneca co.	John H. Camp............................Lyons, Wayne co.
26.—Jonathan B. Morey..............Dansville, Livingston co.	F. O. Mason................................Geneva, Ontario co.
Daniel Morris............................Penn Yan, Yates co.	Furley Holmes............................Penn Yan, Yates co.
27.—William L. Bostwick..............Ithaca, Tompkins co.	Theodore L. Minier..................Binghamton, Broome co.
Gurdon G. Manning................Factoryville, Tioga co.	Alexander E. Andrews...................Avoca, Steuben co.
28.—John N. Hungerford............Corning, Steuben co.	Samuel C. Hoskin.....................Havana, Schuyler co.
Abijah J. Wellman..................Friendship, Allegany co.	Washington Moses....................Granger, Allegany co.
29.—A. Carter Wilder..................Rochester, Monroe co.	Herman Mutcher.....................Rochester, Monroe co.
Dan H. Cole..............................Albion, Orleans co.	John Berry.................................Holley, Orleans co.
30.—Elbert E. Farman................Warsaw, Wyoming co.	John Fisher...............................Batavia, Genesee co.
William Tyrrell.......................Batavia, Genesee co.	Russell C. Mordoff....................Perry, Wyoming co.
31.—John Allen............................Buffalo, Erie co.	Garret B. Hunt..........................Clarence, Erie co.
John Greiner.............................Buffalo, Erie co.	Benjamin Baker......................East Hamburgh, Erie co.
32.—H. O. Lakin..................Jamestown, Chautauqua co.	B. F. Brewer........................Westfield, Chautauqua co.
Henry Van Aernam.........Franklinville, Cattaraugus co.	John Manley....................Little Valley, Cattaraugus co.

NORTH CAROLINA.

AT LARGE.

Thomas Settle..................Douglas, Rockingham co........R. L. Patterson.................Salem, Forsythe co.
Joseph C. Abbott, *Chairman*..........Abbottsburg, Bladen co.......J. A. Hyman.....................Warrenton, Warren co.
Thomas Powers,* *Secretary*...........Newberne, Craven co..........|
James W. Hood..................Charlotte, Mecklenburg co.....W. W. Rollins..................Asheville, Buncombe co.

DISTRICTS.

1.—Louis Hilliard..................Greenville, Pitt co........|
    T. A. Sykes ....Elizabeth City, Pasquotank co....|
2.—George W. Nason, Jr..........Newberne, Craven co........John Robinson..................Goldsboro', Wayne co.
    L. G. Estes.................Enfield, Halifax co........Henry Epps.....................Halifax, Halifax co.
3.—Edward Cantwell............Wilmington, New Hanover co....W. H. Barker..................Pelletier's Mills, Cartaret co.
    George W. Price, Jr.........Wilmington, New Hanover co....R. N. Maultsby................Whitesville, Columbus co.
4.—James H. Harris..............Raleigh, Wake co...........T. F. Lee.......................Raleigh, Wake co.
    J. H. Williamson............Louisburg, Franklin co.....Isaac R. Strayhorne...........Hillsboro, Orange co.
5.—Thomas B. Keogh.............Greensboro', Guilford co....J. Throgmorton................Dobson, Surry co.
    James E. Boyd...............Graham, Alamance co........George M. Arnold..............Greensboro, Guilford co.
6.—John McDonald................Concord, Cabarrus co.......|
    James Sinclair..............Lumberton, Robeson co......|
7.—J. J. Mott...................Catawba Station, Catawba co..D. L. Pringle.................Salisbury, Rowan co.
    George H. Brown.............Wilkesboro', Wilkes co.....|
8.—Pinkney Rollins..............Asheville, Buncombe co.....V. S. Lusk.....................Asheville, Buncombe co.
    E. R. Hampton...............Webster, Jackson co........C. S. Moring...................Old Fort, McDowell co.

OHIO.

AT LARGE.

Jacob Mueller....................Cleveland, Cuyahoga co........S. N. Titus....................Pomeroy, Meigs co.
Samuel Craighead, *Chairman*.....Dayton, Montgomery co.........W. A. Walden..................Steubenville, Jefferson co.
J. Madison Bell..................Toledo, Lucas co..............S. I. Everett.................Cleveland, Cuyahoga co.

OHIO—CONTINUED.

DELEGATES.		ALTERNATES.
AT LARGE.		
Henry Kessler............................Cincinnati	..........Jos. Bruff............	Damascoville, Mahoning co.
R. B. Hayes..............................Cincinnati	..........Robt. Harlan........	..........Cincinnati.
T. W. Sanderson......Youngstown, Mahoning co	..........H. S. Bundy..........	Reed's Mills, Vinton co.

DISTRICTS—(old apportionment.)

1.—James W. Sands......................Cincinnati	..........Gustav Wahle.......	..........Cincinnati.
Henry B. Eckelman..................Cincinnati	..........Charles Kahn........	..........Cincinnati.
2.—Josiah L. Keck........................Cincinnati	..........A. McGill..............	..........Cincinnati.
W. F. Tibballs.........................Cincinnati	..........W. E. Davis..........	..........Cincinnati.
3.—W. D. Bickham............Dayton, Montgomery co	..........Jas. Sayler............	..........Eaton, Preble co.
J. Kelly O'Neil............Lebanon, Warren co	..........John L. Martin......	Dayton, Montgomery co.
4.—Griffith Ellis............Urbana, Champaign co	..........H. H. Darst...........	Tippecanoe, Harrison co.
A. G. Conover................Piqua, Miami co	..........I. Gardner.............	Bellefontaine, Logan co.
5.—David Harpster..........Findley, Hancock co	..........S. H. Hunt.............	Upper Sandusky, Wyandot co.
James L. Price..............Van Wert, Van Wert co	..........—— ——............	
6.—Jeff. Hildebrant........Wilmington, Clinton co	..........B. Sells, Sr.............	Georgetown, Brown co.
A. J. Wright*..............Greenfield, Highland co	..........—— ——............	
7.—Perry Stewart..........Springfield, Clark co	..........C. C. Walcutt........	Columbus, Franklin co.
E. F. Noyes..................Columbus, Franklin co	..........Dan. McMillen......	..........Xenia, Greene co.
8.—John W. Myers..........Mansfield, Richland co	..........J. M. Briggs...........	Mt. Gilead, Morrow co.
S. E. DeWolf....................Marion, Marion co	..........—— ——............	
9.—J. G. Sherman............Wakeman, Huron co	..........John R. Miner.......	..........Sandusky, Erie co.
J. S. York........................Tiffin, Seneca co	..........A. H. Balsley.........	Fremont, Sandusky co.
10.—Wm. Crouse..................Toledo, Lucas co	..........W. D. Beckham.....	..........Napoleon, Henry co.
P. C. Hayes..............Bryan, Williams co	..........Asher Cook...........	Perrysburgh, Wood co.
11.—John B. Gregory..........Portsmouth, Scioto co	..........Jno. G. Peeples......	..........Portsmouth, Scioto co.
W. H. Enochs*............Ironton, Lawrence co	..........—— ——............	
12.—N. J. Turney..........Circleville, Pickaway co	..........George D. Cole......	..........Waverley, Pike co.

DELEGATES AND ALTERNATES. 25

John S. Brasee	Lancaster, Fairfield co	John H. Kelly	New Lexington, Perry co.
13.—Daniel Applegate	Zanesville, Muskingum co	W. C. Fullerton	Newark, Licking co.
W. C. Cooper	Mt. Vernon, Knox co	Jos. Devin	Mt. Vernon, Knox co.
14.—Aaron Pardee	Wadsworth, Medina co		
L. J. Sprengle	Ashland, Ashland co		
15.—N. H. Van Vorhes	Athens, Athens co	H. Horton	Pomeroy, Meigs co.
S. S. Knowles	Marietta, Washington co	F. B. Pond	McConnellsville, Morgan co.
16.—Isaac Welch*		J. L. McIlvaine	New Philadelphia, Tuscarawas co.
W. H. Gooderel	Cambridge, Guernsey co	S. B. Philpot	Summerfield, Noble co.
17.—Wash. Butler	Carrollton, Carroll co	Wm. Robbinson	Steubenville, Jefferson co.
A. W. Williams	Canton, Stark co	Col. —— Morris	New Lisbon, Columbiana co.
18.—John Huntington	Cleveland, Cuyahoga co	Amos Townsend	Cleveland, Cuyahoga co.
Jos. Turney*	Newburgh, Cuyahoga co		
19.—F. G. Servis	Canfield, Mahoning co	C. O. Risden	Ravenna, Portage co.
William M. Eames	Ashtabula, Ashtabula co	T. M. Scott	Chardon, Geauga co.

OREGON.

Hiram Smith	Harrisburg, Linn co		
George P. Holman	Salem, Marion co	*Proxy.*—H. W. Corbett	
Thomas Charman	Oregon City, Clackamas co	*Proxy.*—Myer Hirsch	
B. F. Dowell	Jacksonville, Jackson co	*Proxy.*—H. R. Kincaid	Washington, D. C.
J. P. Booth	Dallas, Polk co		
M. Peterson	Portland, Multnomah co	*Proxy.*—J. F. Devore	

PENNSYLVANIA.

AT LARGE.

Morton McMichael, *Chairman*	Philadelphia	William H. Jessup	Montrose, Susquehanna co.
J. W. F. White	Pittsburgh, Allegheny co	Robert Purvis	Byberry P. O., Philadelphia co.
Henry H. Bingham	Philadelphia	William H. Koontz	Somerset, Somerset co.

PENNSYLVANIA—Continued.

DELEGATES AT LARGE. — ALTERNATES.

Delegate		Alternate	
M. S. Quay	Beaver, Beaver co.	Samuel B. Dick	Meadville, Crawford co.
A. H. Gross	Pittsburgh, Allegheny co.	Sanderson R. Martin	Philadelphia.
David F. Houston	Philadelphia.	William D. Fortin	Philadelphia.

DISTRICTS.

#	Delegate		Alternate	
1.	James N. Kerns	Philadelphia.	William Zane	Philadelphia.
	James Gillingham	Philadelphia.	William Pidgeon	Philadelphia.
2.	George H. Smith*	Philadelphia.	William Calhoran	Philadelphia.
	John A. Shermer	Philadelphia.	Frank Gwynn	Philadelphia.
3.	George Truman, Jr.	Philadelphia.	James C. Kelch	Philadelphia.
	William M. Bunn	Philadelphia.	Edward H. Fitler	Philadelphia.
4.	P. A. B. Widener	Philadelphia.	Thomas Dolan	Philadelphia.
	Charles Thompson Jones	Philadelphia.	William Leacock	Philadelphia.
5.	John Barlow	Philadelphia.	Samuel Sidebotham	Philadelphia.
	Joseph C. Ferguson*	Philadelphia.	John Bromley	Philadelphia.
6.	Josiah Jackson	Kennett Square, Chester co.	H. E. Steele	Coatesville, Chester co.
	William Ward	Chester, Delaware co.	James T. Temple	Darby, Delaware co.
7.	Amos Henderson	Lancaster, Lancaster co.	William G. Case	Columbia, Lancaster co.
	John Strohm	Lancaster, Lancaster co.	R. W. Shenck	Lancaster, Lancaster co.
8.	Samuel Frees	Reading, Berks co.	Harrison Maltzberger	Reading, Berks co.
	William G. Moore	Womelsdorf, Berks co.	William D. Shomo	Hamburg, Berks co.
9.	D. O. Hitner	Norristown, Montgomery co.	James L. Selfridge	Bethlehem, Northampton co.
	John C. Pennington	New Hope, Bucks co.	Jacob Van Buskirk	Milford, Bucks co.
10.	Charles Albright	Mauch Chunk, Carbon co.	John W. Stokes	Stroudsburg, Monroe co.
	John Williamson	Allentown, Lehigh co.	John L. Schreiber	Allentown, Lehigh co.
11.	W. R. Smith	Pottsville, Schuylkill co.	C. F. Shindle	Tamaqua, Schuylkill co.
	M. Whitmoyer	Bloomsburg, Columbia co.	D. A. Beckley	Bloomsburg, Columbia co.
12.	S. F. Barr	Harrisburg, Dauphin co.	C. M. Brown	Harrisburg, Dauphin co.
	George Meily	Lebanon, Lebanon co.	P. Hoopes	Cornwall, Lebanon co.

13.—Joseph A. Scranton	Scranton, Luzerne co	O. F. Gaines	Pittston, Luzerne co.
L. D. Shoemaker	Wilkesbarre, Luzerne co	John McNish	Wilkesbarre, Luzerne co.
14.—N. C. Ellsbra	Towanda, Bradford co	L. F. Fitch	Montrose, Susquehanna co.
P. M. Osterhout	Tunkhannock, Wyoming co	M. A. Rogers	Dushore, Sullivan co.
15.—Robert W. Foresman	Williamsport, Lycoming co	L. H. Kinney	Coudersport, Potter co.
Jerome B. Potter	Wellsboro, Tioga co	John W. Phelps	Coudersport, Potter co.
16.—Edmund Blanchard	Bellefonte, Centre co	A. Wilcox	Benzinger, Elk co.
David W. Woods	Lewistown, Mifflin co	James K. Davis	Selinsgrove, Snyder co.
17.—Samuel McCamant	Tyrone, Blair co	George W. Johnson	Huntingdon, Huntingdon co.
C. T. Roberts	Ebensboro, Cambria co	William C. Roller	Hollidaysburg, Blair co.
18.—George B. Weistling	Chambersburg, Franklin co	John J. Cromer	McConnellsburg, Fulton co.
Joseph Pomeroy	Academia, Juniata co	John M. Krauth	Gettysburg, Adams co.
19.—W. D. Rogers	Waynesburg, Greene co	John J. Worley	Waynesburg, Greene co.
Thomas F. Gallagher	Latrobe, Westmoreland co	W. J. Hitchman	Westmoreland co.
20.—E. B. Brandt	Mechanicsburg, Cumberland co	Peter Ritner	Kerrsville, Cumberland co.
W. H. Shiebley	New Bloomfield, Perry co	John T. Miller	Newport, Perry co.
21.—J. K. Thompson	Indiana, Indiana co	T. S. Wilson	Clarion, Clarion co.
A. G. Henry	Kittanning, Armstrong co	John P. Norman	Clarion, Clarion co.
22.—M. S. Humphries	Pittsburgh, Allegheny co	J. M. Brush	Pittsburgh, Allegheny co.
H. W. Oliver	Pittsburgh, Allegheny co	P. C. Shannon	Pittsburgh, Allegheny co.
23.—James L. Graham	Allegheny, Allegheny co	S. A. Neal	Allegheny, Allegheny co.
H. M. Long	Pittsburgh, Allegheny co	W. J. Gilmore	Pittsburgh, Allegheny co.
24.—C. McCandless	Butler, Butler co	Henry Pillow	Butler, Butler co.
David M. Boyd*	Washington, Washington co	John Hall	Washington, Washington co.
25.—A. B. McCartney	Mercer, Mercer co	S. H. Miller	Mercer, Mercer co.
George K. Anderson	Titusville, Crawford co	James A. Stone	Meadville, Crawford co.
26.—C. W. Gilfillan	Franklin, Venango co	S. V. Holliday	Erie, Erie co.
G. W. Scofield	Warren, Warren co	John A. Dale	Tionesta, Venango co.

DELEGATES AND ALTERNATES.

RHODE ISLAND.

DELEGATES.   ALTERNATES.

Ambrose E. Burnside, *Chairman*......Providence...........————
Thomas M. Seabury*..................Newport.............————
William Goddard*....................Warwick.............————
Edward L. Freeman...................Central Falls.......————
Nelson W. Aldrich...................Providence..........————
Latimer W. Ballou...................Woonsocket..........————
William D. Brayton..................Warwick.............————
Alanson Steere......................Rockland............————

SOUTH CAROLINA.

AT LARGE.

Franklin J. Moses, Jr....Sumpter, Sumpter co......R. A. Cain...............Charleston.
A. J. Ransier............Charleston...............R. H. Gleaves............Beaufort, Beaufort co.

DISTRICTS—(*old apportionment.*)

1.—H. J. Maxwell........Bennettsville, Marlboro' co......J. P. Greene.........Bennettsville, Marlboro' co.
   S. A. Swails........Kingstree, Williamsburg co......————
   F. H. Frost*........Kingstree, Williamsburg co......B. F. Whittemore.....Darlington C. H., Darlington co.
2.—E. W. M. Mackey, *Chairman*......Charleston......J. N. Hayne..........Aiken, Barnwell co.
   Robert Smalls.......Beaufort, Beaufort co......C. D. Hayne..........Aiken, Barnwell co.
   George F. McIntyre..Walterboro, Colleton co......P. P. Hedges.........Charleston.
3.—R. B. Elliott.......Columbia, Richland co......S. J. Lee............Hamburg, Edgefield co.
   W. B. Nash..........Columbia, Richland co......C. M. Wilder.........Columbia, Richland co.
   James L. Orr........Anderson C. H., Anderson co......Lawrence Cain........Edgefield C. H., Edgefield co.
4.—T. J. Mackey........Chester C. H., Chester co......J. S. Mobley.........Union C. H., Union co.
   J. M. Allen.........Greenville, Greenville co......————
   Joseph Crews*.......Laurens C. H., Laurens co......P. J. O'Connell......Fort Mill, York co.

TENNESSEE.

AT LARGE.

David A. Nunn, *Chairman*............Brownsville, Haywood co........Edward Shaw................Memphis, Shelby co.
Henry G. Smith..Memphis, Shelby co........J. C. Stanton..................Chattanooga, Hamilton co.
William Y. Elliott..........................Murfreesboro', Rutherford co........G. W. Blackburn..............Columbia, Maury co.
E. C. Camp*..Knoxville, Knox co........J. A. Dewey...................Dandridge, Jefferson co.
J. A. Hatcher..Somerville, Fayette co........W. A. Newland................Bolivar, Hardeman co.
J. M. Broadnax..Covington, Tipton co........A. Boyd.......................Covington, Tipton co.

DISTRICTS.

1.—R. R. Butler............................Taylorsville, Johnson co.........|
Max. L. Mayer.............................Jonesborough, Washington co........C. P. Toncray................Elizabethtown, Carter co.
2.—A. J. Ricks...............................Knoxville, Knox co........A. S. Prosser................Knoxville, Knox co.
T. M Schlier................................Knoxville, Knox co.........|
3.—Samuel Bard*...|..........W. B. Staley.................Kingston, Roane co.
Henry Deutsch.............................Chattanooga, Hamilton co........A. J. Flowers................Chattanooga, Hamilton co.
4.—W. H. Wisener.......................Shelbyville, Bedford co........William Houston..............Shelbyville, Bedford co.
George E. Grisham*.....................Jonesborough, Washington co........S. D. Mather.................Winchester, Franklin co.
5.—Thomas A. Kercheval*........Nashville, Davidson co.........|
Moses R. Johnson.......................Nashville, Davidson co........Columbus Johnson............Nashville, Davidson co.
6.—J. M. Hill...............................Memphis, Shelby co........R. P. Clark..................Pulaski, Giles co.
D. B. Cliffe..................................Franklin, Williamson co........A. W. Moss...................Franklin, Williamson co.
7.—N. F. Hood............................Clarksville, Montgomery co........Benj. Adkinson...............Clarksville, Montgomery co.
R. M. Thompson........................Huntingdon, Carroll co........James C. Wheeler.............Dover, Stewart co.
8.—W. A. Mabrey........................Brownsville, Haywood co.........|
A. S. Mitchell*...|
9.—Barbour Lewis........................Memphis, Shelby co........James Lott...................Memphis, Shelby co.
Joseph A. Gronauer.....................Somerville, Fayette co........L. E. Dyer...................Memphis, Shelby co.

TEXAS.

DELEGATES. AT LARGE. ALTERNATES.

Webster Flanagan, *Chairman*............Henderson, Rusk co.	William V. Tunstall............	Creswell, Houston co.
A. M. Bryant............Kentuckytown, Grayson co.	A. G. Malloy............	———, Marion co.
G. T. Ruby, *Secretary*............Galveston, Galveston co.	C. L. Abbott............	Hempstead, Austin co.
James P. Newcomb............San Antonio, Bexar co.	Robert Kerr............	Victoria, Victoria co.

DISTRICTS—(*old apportionment.*)

1.—J. B. Williamson............Marshall, Harrison co.	S. H. Russell............	Marshall, Harrison co.
William Chambers............Liberty, Liberty co.	William H. Reynolds............	Liberty, Liberty co.
Thomas Younger............Tyler, Smith co.	————	
2.—W. A. Ellett............Clarksville, Red River co.	————	
Richard Walker*............Dallas, Dallas co.	————	
F. W. Sumner............Sherman, Grayson co.	————	
3.—W. A. Saylor............Bryan, Brazos co.	W. M. Burton............	Richmond, Fort Bend co.
Richard Allen............Houston, Harris co.	A. Zadeck............	Corsicana, Navarro co.
M. V. McMahan............Galveston, Galveston co.	N. W. Curry............	Galveston, Galveston co.
4.—J. W. Talbot............Georgetown, Williamson co.	A. Siemering............	San Antonio, Bexar co.
T. C. Barden............Victoria, Victoria co.	L. D. Camp............	Rockport, Refugio co.
B. F. Williams............Columbus, Colorado co.	J. L. Haynes............	Brownsville, Cameron co.

VERMONT.

AT LARGE.

John Gregory Smith, *Chairman*............St. Albans.	Wheelock G. Veazey............Rutland.
Horace Fairbanks............St. Johnsbury.	John B. Meade............Randolph.
Benj. H. Steele............Hartland.	Asa S. French............St. Johnsbury.
Geo. W. Grandey............Vergennes.	Zadock H. Canfield............Arlington.

DELEGATES AND ALTERNATES.

DISTRICTS.

1.—Geo. A. Tuttle..Rutland........N. T. Sprague, Jr..Brandon.
    George Nichols, *Secretary*..............Northfield........M. S. Colburn.....................................Manchester.
2.—James Hutchinson, Jr......................Randolph........H. R. Stoughton....................................Randolph.
    William Harris, Jr..................................Windham........Clark H. Chapman..............................Proctorsville.
3.—George Wilkins..Stowe........John W. Hartshorn...............................Lunenburg.
    Lawrence Barnes..............................Burlington........Jed. P. Clark..Milton.

VIRGINIA.

AT LARGE.

Edward Daniels...Richmond........C. Y. Thomas..........................Martinsville, Henry co.
H. H. Wells, jr..Richmond........P. G. Thomas......................................Portsmouth.
Charles T. Malord........................Gloucester C. H.......Rufus S. Jones...................................Hampton.
L. H. Chandler...............................Washington, D. C........John Freeman..........................Clover, Halifax co.
Lewis McKenzie.......................................Alexandria........Hector Davis...........................Goochland C. H.
John A. Harman..Staunton........John S. Millson....................................Norfolk.

DISTRICTS—(*old apportionment.*)

1.—Robert Norton..Yorktown........Rufus S. Jones.......................................Hampton.
    P. J. Carter..............................Northampton C. H........F. S. Norton..................................Williamsburg.
2.—J. H. Van Auken..................Stony Creek, Sussex co........Miles Conner..................................Portsmouth.
    R. G. L. Paige...Norfolk........C. W. Tinsley..Norfolk.
3.—John R. Popham, *Chairman*................Richmond........W. H. Lester..Richmond.
    John Robinson.......................Deatonville, Amelia co........R. G. W. Jones............Wilcox Wharf, Elizabeth City co.
4.—Ross Hamilton.....................Boydton, Mecklenburg co........Joseph Davis.........................Pittsylvania C. H.
    M. R. Lloyd......................................Pittsylvania C. H........Joseph C. Russell......................Lawrenceville, Brunswick co.
5.—John Boisseau......................................Lynchburg........J. W. Porter.................................Charlottesville.
    Cæsar Perkins..................................Lynchburg........P. A. Davis.................................Buckingham C. H.

VIRGINIA—CONTINUED.

DELEGATES. | DISTRICTS. | ALTERNATES.

6.—Randolph Martin............................Winchester............George H. Haines...............Winchester.
   C. D. Gray....................................Harrisonburg..........James Cochran..................Staunton.
7.—James B. Sener..............................Fredericksburg........C. H. Bramhall.............Falls Church, Fairfax co.
   Richard H. Lee.........................Warrenton, Fauquier co.....George L. Seaton...............Alexandria.
8.—J. B. Frier...............................Salem, Roanoke co.......John W. Woltz..................Richmond.
   G. G. Goodell............................Marion, Smyth co........Geo. H. Smith.............Marion, Smyth co.

WEST VIRGINIA.

DISTRICTS.

1.—W. E. Stevenson, *Chairman*............Parkersburg, Wood co........J. W. Allison..................Hancock co.
   R. W. Simmons.........................Parkersburg, Wood co........W. L. Cole..............West Union, Doddridge co.
   George Edwards.......................Moundsville, Marshall co......J. M. Pipes...............Moundsville, Marshall co.
   C. F. Scott.............................Harrisville, Ritchie co........R. S. Northcott...........Clarksburg, Harrison co.
2.—D. D. T. Farnsworth.....................Buckannon, Upshur co.......A. C. Moore..............Clarksburg, Harrison co.
   J. M. Hagans, *Secretary*...........Morgantown, Monongolia co....J. T. Hoke................New Creek, Mineral co.
   Charles Hooton........................Rowlesburg, Preston co.......Wm. Smith................Martinsburg, Berkeley co.
3.—T. B. Swann..........................Charleston, Kanawha co.......George Koonce............Harper's Ferry, Jefferson co.
   R. A. Burnap....................Point Pleasant, Mason co......William O. Wright.......Cabell Court-House, Cabell co.
   John E. Schley.....................Shepherdstown, Jefferson co....George W. Moredock.....Point Pleasant, Mason co.

WISCONSIN.

AT LARGE.

Lucius Fairchild.............................Madison, Dane co..........E. S. Miner..................Necedah, Juneau co.
C. J. L. Meyer.........................Fond du Lac, Fond du Lac co...A. M. Thompson..........Milwaukee, Milwaukee co.
Thomas S. Allen......................Oshkosh, Winnebago co.......H. S. Sackett.............Berlin, Green Lake co.
James Bintliff..........................Janesville, Rock co..........A. S. Barnes.............Delavan, Walworth co.

DELEGATES AND ALTERNATES.

DISTRICTS.

1.—L. S. Blake..................................Racine, Racine co........A. E. Gilbert..................................Waukesha, Waukesha co.
    Frank Leland..............................Elkhorn, Walworth co......Mark Dresser.................................Kenosha, Kenosha co.
2.—N. S. Green................................Milford, Jefferson co......C. H. Phillips..............................Lake Mills, Jefferson co.
    E. W. Keyes, *Chairman*.............Madison, Dane co........George Griswold........................Columbus, Columbia co.
3.—G. W. Ryland..............................Lancaster, Grant co......W. H. Brisbane..........................Arena, Iowa co.
    A. Ludlow....................................Monroe, Greene co......Wilson Ladue............................La Fayette, La Fayette co.
4.—Asahel Finch..............................Milwaukee, Milwaukee co......L. A. Proctor..........................Milwaukee, Milwaukee co.
    L. F. Frisby................................West Bend, Washington co......E. S. Turner.........................Port Washington, Ozaukee co.
5.—John H. Jones, *Secretary*..........Sheboygan, Sheboygan co......Conrad Krez..........................Sheboygan, Sheboygan co.
    Otto Troemels...........................Manitowoc, Manitowoc co......J. B. Perry...........................Fond du Lac, Fond du Lac co.
6.—George M. Paine........................Oshkosh, Winnebago co......C. S. Ogden...........................Waupacca, Waupacca co.
    W. H. H. Wroe...........................Medina, Outagamie co......George Grimmer....................Ahnapee, Kewaunee co.
7.—J. G. Thorpe..............................Eau Claire, Eau Claire co......R. May.................................Springville, Vernon co.
    John Comstock..........................Hudson, St. Croix co......O. S. Powell..........................River Falls, Pierce co.
8.—Walter D. McIndoe.....................Wausan, Marathon co......George A. Newes...................Grand Rapids, Wood co.
    Thaddeus C. Pound....................Chippewa Falls, Chippewa co......M. H. McCord....................Shawanaw, Shawanaw co.

TERRITORIES.

ARIZONA.

DELEGATES.		ALTERNATES.
John Titus	Tucson	
James H. Toole	Tucson	

COLORADO.

Jerome B. Chaffee	Central City	William Hardin...Denver.
George M. Chillicothe	Denver	C. J. Martin...Burlington.

DAKOTA.

[Entitled to two votes; four delegates admitted.]

J. H. Burdick	Yankton	Newton Clark...Sioux Falls.
Alexander Hughes	Elk Point	John L. Taylor...Vermillion.
Laban H. Litchfield	Yankton	N. E. Phillips...Sioux Falls.
John G. Meade	Bonhomie	J. P. Kidder...Vermillion.

DISTRICT OF COLUMBIA.

Alexander R. Shepherd	Washington	F. A. Boswell...Washington.
John F. Cooke	Washington	A. M. Green...Washington.

IDAHO.

E. J. Curtis		
John R. McBride*		

MONTANA.

Wilbur F. Sanders..................Helena......Jasper A. Viall..................Helena.
Lucius B. Church..................Helena......Lester S. Wilson.................Bozeman.

NEW MEXICO.

Marsh Giddings..................Santa Fé......————..................————
J. G. Palen.....................Santa Fé......*Proxy.*—William Breeden.........Santa Fé.

UTAH.

[*Elected at the Republican Convention holden at Salt Lake, April 5, and rejected by the Convention.*]

Thomas Fitch....................Salt Lake......George Smith....................Salt Lake.
Frank Fuller....................Salt Lake......William Jennings................Salt Lake.

[*Elected at the Republican Convention holden at Corrinne, May 16, and admitted by the Convention.*]

A. S. Gould.....................Salt Lake......Dennis J. Toohy.................Corrinne.
O. J. Hollister.................Corrinne......Oscar G. Sawyer.................Salt Lake.

WASHINGTON.

James McNaught*.................Seatle......————..................————
Lyman B. Andrews................Seatle......————..................————

WYOMING.

G. W. Corey*....................Cheyenne, Laramie co......J. A. Campbell..........Cheyenne, Laramie co.
J. W. Donnellan.................Laramie City, Albany co...J. W. Hugus............Fort Steele, Carbon co.

Number of Delegates to which each State and Territory was entitled, under the call of the National Committee.

States.		States.	
Alabama	20	Ohio	44
Arkansas	12	Oregon	6
California	12	Pennsylvania	58
Connecticut	12	Rhode Island	8
Delaware	6	South Carolina	14
Florida	8	Tennessee	24
Georgia	22	Texas	16
Illinois	42	Vermont	10
Indiana	30	Virginia	22
Iowa	22	West Virginia	10
Kansas	10	Wisconsin	20
Kentucky	24		
Louisiana	16	**Territories.**	
Maine	14	Arizona	2
Maryland	16	Colorado	2
Massachusetts	26	Dakota	2
Michigan	22	District of Columbia	2
Minnesota	10	Idaho	2
Mississippi	16	Montana	2
Missouri	30	New Mexico	2
Nebraska	6	Utah	2
Nevada	6	Washington	2
New Hampshire	10	Wyoming	2
New Jersey	18		
New York	70	Total	752
North Carolina	20		

Number of electors, 366; majority of electoral votes, **184.**

OFFICIAL NOTIFICATION

OF

President Grant and Senator Wilson

BY THE

OFFICERS OF THE CONVENTION,

Washington, D. C., June 10, 1872.

The President and Vice-Presidents of the National Republican Convention, at half-past one o'clock to-day, proceeded in a body to the Executive Mansion to formally and officially notify the President of his nomination by the Republican party for the office of President of the United States for the term ending March 4, 1877.

On reaching the Executive Mansion, they were shown into the President's private parlor. The President immediately came in, and was personally introduced to each member of the official party by Hon. Thomas Settle, who presided over the Convention.

The ceremony of introduction over, Mr. Settle addressed the President as follows:

Mr. President: We visit you to-day for the purpose of performing a very agreeable duty. We come to officially inform you of your unanimous nomination for the Presidency by the National Republican Convention assembled in Philadelphia on the 6th instant. Beyond making this formal announcement, I do not know that we have anything to add.

Mr. Settle then handed the President the following official letter, signed by the officers of the Convention:

WASHINGTON, D. C., *June 10*, 1872.

To the President:

SIR: In pursuance of our instructions, we, the undersigned, President and Vice-Presidents of the National Republican Convention held in Philadelphia on the 5th and 6th instant, have the honor to inform you of your nomination for re-election to the office of President of the United States.

As it is impossible to give an adequate idea of the enthusiasm which prevailed, or the unanimity which hailed you as the choice of the people, we can only add that you received the entire vote of every State and Territory.

Regarding your re-election as necessary to the peace and continued prosperity of the country, we ask your acceptance of the nomination.

THOMAS SETTLE,
President National Republican Convention.

VICE-PRESIDENTS.

Paul Strobach, Alabama.
Elisha Baxter, Arkansas.
H. S. Sargent, California.
Sabin L. Sayles, Connecticut.
Isaac Jump, Delaware.
Benjamin Conley, Georgia.
Emery A. Storrs, Illinois.
Sol. D. Meredith, Indiana.
W. H. Seevers, Iowa.
John C. Carpenter, Kansas.
R. M. Kelly, Kentucky.
Lewis Trager, Louisiana.
Frederick Robie, Maine.
Thomas Kelso, Maryland.
A. H. Rice, Massachusetts.
E. B. Ward, Michigan.
C. T. Benedict, Minnesota.
R. W. Flourney, Mississippi.
J. F. Benjamin, Missouri.
John S. Bowen, Nebraska.
Wm. H. Y. Hackett, New Hampshire.
Douglass S. Gregory, New Jersey.
H. B. Claflin, New York.
Edward Cantwell, North Carolina.
Jacob C. Muehler, Ohio.
John P. Booth, Oregon.
H. W. Oliver, Pennsylvania.
A. E. Burnside, Rhode Island.
A. J. Ransier, South Carolina.
Wm. H. Wisener, Tennessee.
A. B. Norton, Texas.
H. Fairbanks, Vermont.
Chas. T. Malord, Virginia.
Chas. Hooton, West Virginia.
Lucius Fairchild, Wisconsin.
Dennis Egan, Florida.
Geo. M. Chillicothe, Colorado.
John F. Cook, District of Columbia.
John R. McBride, Idaho.
John W. Donnellan, Wyoming.
O. J. Hollister, Utah.
Wm. Breeden, New Mexico.
L. B. Church, Montana.

The President received the letter, and bowing, said:

Well, gentlemen, at present I am not prepared to fully respond to your letter, but will do so soon.

Judge SETTLE. Thank you, sir.

Mr. STORRS, of Illinois. I wish the President of the Convention would tell President Grant what a superb Convention we had, and how we have never seen anything that equalled it.

Judge SETTLE. My friend is aware that it is not my habit to make a speech, and I confess I do not feel equal to the task he suggests.

The PRESIDENT. That is a speech I like. I can respond to that. It is short and to the point. [Laughter.]

Judge SETTLE. Nothing is more certain than that I should fail if I attempted anything like a description of the Convention. Mere words cannot do the subject justice. The enthusiasm, the unanimity, the solid vote of every State, the good feeling pervading the entire Convention, cannot be adequately described, and has not been, even in the public prints. In order to fully appreciate the Convention, the President himself should have been present. What we now desire especially to do is to tell the President what we mean to accomplish in November.

Mr. STROBACH, of Alabama. As a representative of the Germans of America, I not only pledge the State of Alabama for you in November by a handsome majority, but I pledge you the overwhelming vote of 800,000 Germans in the United States.

The PRESIDENT. It is sincerely gratifying to me to know that after holding for three years the exalted office I now occupy, and without any political training whatever, I am again endorsed by kind friends and former supporters. I am, of course, deeply grateful.

General SOLOMON D. MEREDITH. A single word here is appropriate. The nomination of President Grant is unprecedented in all the history of the United States. Every congressional district in Pennsylvania was represented in the Convention, and every vote was cast for you, Mr. President. Never have I seen before in a nominating convention such unanimity as was exhibited at Philadelphia. It is very flattering to you, sir; and now let me say for Indiana that she will give you her fifteen electoral votes. I'll say nothing now as to the precise majority, but of the State you may be sure.

The PRESIDENT. At any rate, General, don't let your people vote but once each. [Laughter.]

General MEREDITH. No; we shall give you the State by a handsome majority by allowing each man to vote once only.

OFFICIAL NOTIFICATION.

Similar assurances were made to the President by different members of the delegation assenting in a word or two to what General Meredith had said.

Mr. STORRS. The endorsement of General Grant at Philadelphia is the endorsement of a man with good and honest purposes, and my State of Illinois proposes to give him a majority next November of from 30,000 to 50,000.

General JOHN F. BENJAMIN, of Missouri. You are as well aware, Mr. President, as I am, that disaffection has existed in the ranks of the Republican party in Missouri, but we hope to give its electoral vote for Grant and Wilson.

Governor Fairchild, of Wisconsin, followed General Benjamin, pledging the State of Wisconsin, and similar pledges were made by the representative from Michigan and by Mr. Malord, of Virginia.

Mr. A. B. NORTON, of Texas. *Mr. President:* Every true and loyal man in Texas will give you a cordial support, and for the reason that no loyal man can live in Texas unless he has about him the strong, protecting arm of the Government. We propose to do now what we did in 1868, and our whole duty will be done at the polls. If Horace Greeley is nominated at Baltimore, Texas will give her electoral vote to President Grant.

Mr. W. H. WISENER, of Tennessee. *Mr. President:* It is a great pleasure to me to promise you that we will make in your behalf a gallant fight in Tennessee. There are many Democrats in my State who, if called upon to give up their organization to Greeley and Brown, will prefer to capitulate to you, as they did in 1865.

This closed the congratulatory speech-making. The President then again informed the committee that he would read their letter, and respond in writing.

The delegation then withdrew.

Subsequently the President's letter was received, as follows:

EXECUTIVE MANSION,
WASHINGTON, D. C., *June* 10, 1872.

Hon. THOMAS SETTLE, *President National Republican Convention;* PAUL STROBACH, ELISHA A. BAXTER, H. S. SARGENT, and others, *Vice-Presidents:*

GENTLEMEN: Your letter of this date, advising me of the action of the Convention held in Philadelphia, Pennsylvania, on the 5th and 6th of this month, and of my unanimous nomination for the Presidency by it, is received.

I accept the nomination, and through you return my heartfelt thanks to your constituents for this mark of their confidence and support.

If elected in November and protected by a kind Providence in health and strength to perform the duties of the high trust conferred, I promise the same zeal and devotion to the good of the whole people for the future of my official life as shown in the past.

Past experience may guide me in avoiding mistakes inevitable with novices in all professions and in all occupations.

When relieved from the responsibilities of my present trust, by the election of a successor, whether it be at the end of this term or the next, I hope to leave to him, as Executive, a country at peace within its own borders, at peace with outside nations, with a credit at home and abroad, and without embarrassing questions to threaten its future prosperity.

With the expression of a desire to see a speedy healing of all bitterness of feeling between sections, parties, or races of citizens, and the time when the title of *citizen* carries with it all the protection and privileges to the humblest that it does to the most exalted, I subscribe myself, very respectfully, your obedient servant,

U. S. GRANT.

After the delegation left the Executive Mansion they proceeded to the Capitol, and assembled in the room of the Committee on Military Affairs. Senator Wilson having entered, Mr. Settle said that they had a pleasing duty to perform in acquainting him with his nomination for the Vice-Presidency of the United States, and also in presenting him with the official letter of the Convention.

Senator WILSON made the following impromptu reply:

SENATOR WILSON'S REPLY.

I will in a day or two give you an answer in writing to this communication. I take this occasion, however, to thank you and the members of the Convention you represent for this manifestation of your confidence. As I neither asked nor wrote to any member of the Convention to give me a vote, I am the more grateful for their generous support. I am grateful, too, for the friendly tone of the Republican press of the country. For thirty years, in public and in private life, I have striven to maintain the distinguishing idea of the Republican party—the freedom and equality of all men. I have striven to be true to my country, and to the rights of our common humanity; to know no sectional interest, nor race, nor color. In the future, as in the past, I shall unfalteringly adhere to the principles which are the convictions of my judgment, heart, and conscience.

I am clearly of the opinion that the great soldier who rendered such illustrious services to the country in the great civil war will be re-elected President of the United States. His humanity to the vanquished, his firmness in vindicating the rights of the humble and defenceless, and his devotion to the leading ideas of the Republican party, cannot be questioned. I esteem it a high honor to be associated with him in the coming contest.

While I am grateful to the friends who gave me such generous support, I honor those who adhered with so much devotion to Mr. Colfax. We have been personal and political friends for nearly twenty years, and it is a source of profound satisfaction to me that our personal relations have not been disturbed by the recent contest. While I shall never cease to feel grateful to friends who honored me by their support, I shall ever entertain sincere respect for those who deemed it to be their duty to give their support to others. I hope we shall all strive to win to our support every honest and patriotic man in the country; every man true to the rights of humanity; every man who would elevate the condition of the toiling millions and have our Republic become a great Christian nation, an example to the world.

Let it be understood that our ranks are wide open to receive all devoted to the country, and who would advance the happiness and general well-being of all sections of the land and all conditions of the people. We Republicans should offer the hand of reconciliation to all fair-minded and honorable men, and use all legitimate means to achieve success for the honor and salvation of the country, as well as for that of the party which saved the Union and established freedom in every part of the land.

SENATOR WILSON'S LETTER OF ACCEPTANCE.

WASHINGTON, *June* 14.

Hon. THOMAS SETTLE, *President of the National Republican Convention;* PAUL STROBACH, ELISHA BAXTER, H. S. SARGENT, and others, *Vice-Presidents:*

GENTLEMEN: Your note of the 10th instant, conveying to me the action of the Convention in placing my name in nomination for the office of Vice-President of the United States, is before me. I need not give you an assurance of my grateful appreciation of the high honor conferred on me by this action of the fifth National Convention of the Republican party.

Sixteen years ago, in the same city, was held the first meeting of men who, amid the darkness and doubts of that hour of slave-holding ascendancy and aggression, had assembled in national convention to confer with each other on the exigencies to which that fearful domination had brought their country. After a full conference, the highest point of resolve they could reach, the most they dared to recommend, was the avowed purpose to prohibit the existence of slavery in the Territories.

Last week the same party met by its representatives from thirty-seven States and ten Territories, at the same great centre of wealth, intelligence, and power, to review the past, take note of the present, and indicate its line of action for the future. As typical facts of the headlands of the nation's recent history, there sat on its platform, taking a prominent and honorable part in its proceedings, admitted on terms of perfect equality to the leading hotels of the city, not only colored representatives of the race which was ten years before in abject slavery, but one of the oldest and most prominent of the once despised abolitionists, to whom was accorded, as to no other, the warmest demonstration of popular regard and esteem, an ovation not to him alone, but to the cause he had for so many years represented, and to the men and women, living and dead, who had toiled through long years of obliquity and self-sacrifice for the glorious fruition of that hour. It hardly needed a brilliant summary of its platform to set forth its illustrious achievements. The very presence of those men was alone significant of victories already achieved, the progress already made, and the great distance which the nation had travelled between the years 1856 and 1872.

But grand as had been its record, the Republican party rests not on its past alone; it looks to the future and grapples with its problems of duty and danger. It proposes, as objects of its immediate accomplishment, complete liberty and exact equality for all, the enforcement of the recent amendments to the National Constitution, reform in the civil service, the national domain to be set apart for homes for the people, the adjustment of duties on imports so as to secure remunerative wages to labor, the extension of bounties to all soldiers and sailors who, in the line of duty, become disabled, continued and careful encouragement and protection to voluntary immigration, and guarding with zealous care the rights of the adopted citizens, the abolition of the franking privilege, and the speedy reduction of the national debt and the rates of interest, and the resumption of specie payment, the encouragement of American commerce and of ship-building, the suppression of violence, and protection of the ballot-box. It also placed on record the opinion and purposes of the party in favor of amnesty, against all forms of repudiation, and endorsed the humane and peaceful policy of the Administration in regard to the Indians.

But while clearly defining and distinctly announcing the policy of the Republican party on these questions of practical legislation and administration, the Convention did not ignore the great social problems which are pressing their claims for solution, and which demand the most careful study and wise consideration. Foremost stands the labor question, concerning the relations of capital and labor. The Republican party accepts the duty of so shaping legislation as to secure a full protection and amplest field for capital, and for labor, the creation of capital, the largest opportunities and a just share of the mutual profits of these two great servants of civilization. To woman, too, and her new demands, it extends the hand of grateful recognition and proffers its most respectful inquiry. It recognizes her noble devotion to the country and freedom, welcomes her admission to wider fields of usefulness, and commends her demands for additional rights to the calm and careful consideration of the nation. To guard well what has already been secured, to work out faithfully and wisely what is now in hand, and to consider questions which are looming up to view but a little way before us, the Republican party is to-day what it was in the gloomy years of slavery, rebellion, and reconstruction—a national necessity.

It appeals, therefore, for support to the patriotic and liberty-loving, to the just and humane, to all who would dignify labor, to all who would educate, elevate, and lighten the burdens of the sons and daughters of toil. With its great record, the work still to be done under the great soldier whose historic renown and whose successful administration for the last three years begot such popular confidence, the Republican party may confidently, in the language of the Convention you represent, start on a new march to victory.

Having accepted for thirty-six years of my life the distinguishing doctrines of the Republican party of to-day; having, during years of that period, for their advancement subordinated all other issues, acting in and co-operating with political organizations with whose leading doctrines I sometimes had neither sympathy nor belief; having labored incessantly for many years to found and build up the Republican party, and having during its existence taken an humble part in the grand work, I gratefully accept the nomination thus tendered, and shall endeavor, if it shall be ratified by the people, faithfully to perform the duties it imposes.

Respectfully yours,

HENRY WILSON.

National Union Republican Conventions.

CALLS AND PLATFORMS.

PLATFORM ADOPTED AT PHILADELPHIA, 1856.

This convention of delegates, assembled in pursuance of a call addressed to the people of the United States, without regard to past political differences or divisions, who are opposed to the repeal of the Missouri compromise, to the policy of the present Administration, to the extension of slavery into free territory, in favor of admitting Kansas as a free State, of restoring the action of the Federal Government to the principles of Washington and Jefferson, and who purpose to unite in presenting candidates for the offices of President and Vice-President, do resolve as follows:

1. That the maintenance of the principles promulgated in the Declaration of Independence and embodied in the Federal Constitution is essential to the preservation of our republican institutions, and that the Federal Constitution, the rights of the States, and the union of the States, shall be preserved; that, with our republican fathers, we hold it to be a self-evident truth, that all men are endowed with the inalienable rights to life, liberty, and the pursuit of happiness, and that the primary object and ulterior design of our Federal Government were to secure these rights to all persons within its exclusive jurisdiction; that, as our republican fathers, when they had abolished slavery in all our national territory, ordained that no person should be deprived of life, liberty, or property without due process of law, it becomes our duty to maintain this provision of the Constitution against all attempts to violate it for the purpose of establishing slavery in the United States by positive legislation prohibiting its existence or extension therein; that we deny the authority of Congress, of a territorial legislature, of any individual or association of individuals, to give legal existence to slavery in any Territory of the United States while the present Constitution shall be maintained.

2. That the Constitution confers upon Congress sovereign power over the Territories of the United States for their government, and that in the exercise of this power it is both the right and the duty of Congress to prohibit in the Territories those twin relics of barbarism—polygamy and slavery.

3. That, while the Constitution of the United States was ordained and established by the people "in order to form a more perfect union, establish justice, insure domestic tranquillity, provide for the common defence,

promote the general welfare, and secure the blessings of liberty," and contains ample provisions for the protection of the life, liberty, and property of every citizen, the dearest constitutional rights of the people of Kansas have been fraudulently and violently taken from them; their territory has been invaded by an armed force; spurious and pretended legislative, judicial, and executive officers have been set over them, by whose usurped authority, sustained by the military power of the Government, tyrannical and unconstitutional laws have been enacted and enforced; the right of the people to keep and bear arms has been infringed; test-oaths of an extraordinary and entangling nature have been imposed as a condition of exercising the right of suffrage and holding office; the right of an accused person to a speedy and public trial by an impartial jury has been denied; the right of the people to be secure in their persons, houses, papers, and effects, against unreasonable searches and seizures, has been violated; they have been deprived of life, liberty, and property without due process of law; that the freedom of speech and of the press has been abridged; the right to choose their representatives has been made of no effect; murders, robberies, and arsons have been instigated and encouraged, and the offenders have been allowed to go unpunished; that all these things have been done with the knowledge, sanction, and procurement of the present Administration, and that for this high crime against the Constitution, the Union, and humanity, we arraign the Administration, the President, his advisers, agents, supporters, apologists, and accessories either *before* or *after* the fact, before the country and before the world; and that it is our fixed purpose to bring the actual perpetrators of these atrocious outrages and their accomplices to a sure and condign punishment hereafter.

4. That Kansas should be immediately admitted as a State of the Union, with her present free constitution, as at once the most effectual way of securing to her citizens the enjoyment of the rights and privileges to which they are entitled, and of ending the civil strife now raging in her territory.

5. That the highwayman's plea that "might makes right," embodied in the Ostend circular, was in every respect unworthy of American diplomacy, and would bring shame and dishonor upon any Government or people that gave it their sanction.

6. That a railroad to the Pacific Ocean by the most central and practicable route is imperatively demanded by the interests of the whole country, and that the Federal Government ought to render immediate and efficient aid in its construction; and, as an auxiliary thereto, to the immediate construction of an emigrant route on the line of the railroad.

7. That appropriations by Congress for the improvement of rivers and harbors of a national character, required for the accommodation and security of our existing commerce, are authorized by the Constitution and justified by the obligation of Government to protect the lives and property of its citizens.

8. That we invite the affiliation and co-operation of freemen of all parties, however differing from us in other respects, in support of the principles herein declared; and, believing that the spirit of our institutions, as well as the Constitution of our country, guarantees liberty of conscience and equality of rights among citizens, we oppose all legislation impairing their security.

Call for the Convention at Chicago, 1860.

A National Republican Convention will meet at Chicago, on Wednesday, the 13th day of June next, at 12 o'clock, noon, for the nomination of candidates to be supported for President and Vice-President at the next election.

The Republican electors of the several States, the members of the People's party of Pennsylvania and of the Opposition party of New Jersey, and all others who are willing to co-operate with them in support of the candidates who shall there be nominated, and who are opposed to the policy of the present Administration; to Federal corruption and usurpation; to the extension of slavery into the Territories; to the new and dangerous political doctrine that the Constitution, of its own force, carries slavery into all the Territories of the United States; to the reopening of the African slave trade; to any inequality of rights among citizens; and who are in favor of the immediate admission of Kansas into the Union under the constitution recently adopted by its people; of restoring the Federal Administration to a system of rigid economy, and to the principles of Washington and Jefferson; of maintaining inviolate the rights of the States and defending the soil of every State and Territory from lawless invasion; and of preserving the integrity of this Union and the supremacy of the Constitution, and laws passed in pursuance thereof, against the conspiracy of the leaders of a sectional party to resist the majority principle as established in this Government at the expense of its existence, are invited to send from each State two delegates from every Congressional district and four delegates at large to the Convention.

EDWIN D. MORGAN, N. Y.
JOSEPH BARTLETT, Me.
GEORGE G. FOGG, N. H.
LAWRENCE BRAINERD, Vt.
JOHN T. GOODRICH, Mass.
WM. M. CHASE, R. I.
GIDEON WELLES, Conn.
THOMAS WILLIAMS, Penn.
GEORGE HARRIS, Md.
ALFRED CALDWELL, Va.
THOMAS SPOONER, Ohio.
CASSIUS M. CLAY, Ky.
JAMES RITCHIE, Ind.
NORMAN B. JUDD, Ill.
ZACHARIAH CHANDLER, Mich.
JOHN H. TWEEDY, Wis.
ALEXANDER H. RAMSEY, Minn.
ANDREW J. STEVENS, Iowa.
ASA S. JONES, Mo.
MARTIN F. CONWAY, Kan.
LEWIS CLEPHANE, D. C.

Platform Adopted at Chicago, 1860.

Resolved, That we, the delegated representatives of the Republican electors of the United States, in convention assembled, in discharge of the duty we owe to our constituents and our country, unite in the following declarations:

1. That the history of the nation, during the last four years, has fully established the propriety and necessity of the organization and perpetuation of the Republican party, and that the causes which called it into existence are permanent in their nature, and now, more than ever before, demand its peaceful and constitutional triumph.

2. That the maintenance of the principles promulgated in the Declaration of Independence and embodied in the Federal Constitution, "that

all men are created equal; that they are endowed by their Creator with certain inalienable rights; that among these are life, liberty, and the pursuit of happiness; that to secure these rights governments are instituted among men, deriving their just powers from the consent of the governed," is essential to the preservation of our republican institutions; and that the Federal Constitution, the rights of the States, and the union of the States must and shall be preserved.

3. That to the union of the States this nation owes its unprecedented increase in population, its surprising development of material resources, its rapid augmentation of wealth, its happiness at home, and its honor abroad; and we hold in abhorrence all schemes for disunion, come from whatever source they may: and we congratulate the country that no Republican member of Congress has uttered or countenanced the threats of disunion so often made by Democratic members without rebuke, and with applause from their political associates; and we denounce those threats of disunion, in case of a popular overthrow of their ascendancy, as denying the vital principles of a free government, and as an avowal of contemplated treason which it is the imperative duty of an indignant people sternly to rebuke and forever silence.

4. That the maintenance inviolate of the rights of the States, and especially the right of each State to order and control its own domestic institutions according to its own judgment exclusively, is essential to that balance of power on which the perfection and endurance of our political fabric depends; and we denounce the lawless invasion by armed force of the soil of any State or Territory, no matter under what pretext, as among the gravest of crimes.

5. That the present Democratic Administration has far exceeded our worst apprehensions, in its measureless subserviency to the exactions of a sectional interest, as especially evinced in its desperate exertions to force the infamous Lecompton constitution upon the protesting people of Kansas; in construing the personal relation between master and servant to involve an unqualified property in persons; in its attempted enforcement everywhere, on land and sea, through the intervention of Congress and of the Federal courts, of the extreme pretensions of a purely local interest; and in its general and unvarying abuse of the power entrusted to it by a confiding people.

6. That the people justly view with alarm the reckless extravagance which pervades every department of the Federal Government. That a return to rigid economy and accountability is indispensable to arrest the systematic plunder of the public treasury by favored partisans; while the recent startling developments of frauds and corruptions at the Federal metropolis show that an entire change of administration is imperatively demanded.

7. That the new dogma that the Constitution, of its own force, carries slavery into any or all of the Territories of the United States, is a dangerous political heresy, at variance with the explicit provisions of that instrument itself, with contemporaneous exposition, and with legislative and judicial precedent; is revolutionary in its tendency, and subversive of the peace and harmony of the country.

8. That the normal condition of all the territory of the United States is that of freedom; that as our republican fathers, when they had abolished slavery in all our national territory, ordained "that no person

should be deprived of life, liberty, or property without due process of law," it becomes our duty, by legislation, whenever such legislation is necessary, to maintain this provision of the Constitution against all attempts to violate it; and we deny the authority of Congress, of a territorial legislature, or of any individuals, to give legal existence to slavery in any Territory of the United States.

9. That we brand the recent re-opening of the African slave trade, under the cover of our national flag, aided by perversions of judicial power, as a crime against humanity and a burning shame to our country and age; and we call upon Congress to take prompt and efficient measures for the total and final suppression of that execrable traffic.

10. That in the recent vetoes, by their Federal Governors, of the acts of the legislatures of Kansas and Nebraska, prohibiting slavery in those Territories, we find a practical illustration of the boasted democratic principle of non-intervention and popular sovereignty, embodied in the Kansas-Nebraska bill, and a demonstration of the deception and fraud involved therein.

11. That Kansas should, of right, be immediately admitted as a State under the constitution recently formed and adopted by her people and accepted by the House of Representatives.

12. That while providing revenue for the support of the General Government by duties upon imports, sound policy requires such an adjustment of these imposts as to encourage the development of the industrial interest of the whole country; and we commend that policy of national exchanges which secures to the workingmen liberal wages, to agriculture remunerating prices, to mechanics and manufacturers an adequate reward for their skill, labor, and enterprise, and to the nation commercial prosperity and independence.

13. That we protest against any sale or alienation to others of the public lands held by actual settlers, and against any view of the free homestead policy which regards the settlers as paupers or suppliants for public bounty; and we demand the passage by Congress of the complete and satisfactory homestead measure which has already passed the House.

14. That the Republican party is opposed to any change in our naturalization laws, or any State legislation, by which the rights of citizenship hitherto accorded to immigrants from foreign lands shall be abridged or impaired; and in favor of giving a full and efficient protection to the rights of all classes of citizens, whether native or naturalized, both at home and abroad.

15. That appropriations by Congress for river and harbor improvements of a national character, required for the accommodation and security of an existing commerce, are authorized by the Constitution and justified by the obligation of Government to protect the lives and property of its citizens.

16. That a railroad to the Pacific Ocean is imperatively demanded by the interests of the whole country; that the Federal Government ought to render immediate and efficient aid in its construction, and that, as preliminary thereto, a daily overland mail should be promptly established.

17. Finally, having thus set forth our distinctive principles and views, we invite the co-operation of all citizens, however differing on other questions, who substantially agree with us in their affirmance and support.

CALL FOR THE CONVENTION AT BALTIMORE, 1864.

The undersigned, who by original appointment, or subsequent designation to fill vacancies, constitute the executive committee created by the National Convention held at Chicago on the 16th day of May, 1860, do hereby call upon all qualified voters who desire the unconditional maintenance of the Union, the supremacy of the Constitution, and the complete suppression of the existing rebellion, with the cause thereof, by vigorous war and all apt and efficient means, to send delegates to a convention to assemble at Baltimore, on Tuesday, the 7th day of June, 1864, at 12 o'clock, noon, for the purpose of presenting candidates for the offices of President and Vice-President of the United States. Each State having a representation in Congress will be entitled to as many delegates as shall be equal to twice the number of electors to which such State is entitled in the electoral college of the United States.

EDWIN D. MORGAN, N. Y.,
    Chairman.
CHARLES J. GILMAN, Me.
E. H. ROLLINS, N. H.
L. BRAINERD, Vt.
J. Z. GOODRICH, Mass.
THOMAS G. TURNER, R. I.
GIDEON WELLES, Conn.
DENNING DUER, N. J.
EDWARD McPHERSON, Penn.
N. B. SMITHERS, Del.
J. F. WAGNER, Md.
THOMAS SPOONER, Ohio.
H. S. LANE, Ind.
SAMUEL L. CASEY, Ky.
E. PECK, Ill.
HERBERT M. HOXIE, Iowa.
AUSTIN BLAIR, Mich.
CARL SCHURZ, Wis.
W. D. WASHBURN, Minn.
CORNELIUS COLE, Cal.
WM. A. PHILLIPS, Kan.
O. H. IRISH, Neb.
JOS. GERHARDT, D. C.

WASHINGTON, *February* 22, 1864.

PLATFORM ADOPTED AT BALTIMORE, 1864.

1. *Resolved*, That it is the highest duty of every American citizen to maintain against all their enemies the integrity of the Union and the paramount authority of the Constitution and laws of the United States; and that, laying aside all differences of political opinion, we pledge ourselves, as Union men, animated by a common sentiment and aiming at a common object, to do everything in our power to aid the Government in quelling by force of arms the rebellion now raging against its authority, and in bringing to the punishment due to their crimes the rebels and traitors arrayed against it.

2. *Resolved*, That we approve the determination of the Government of the United States not to compromise with the rebels, or to offer them any terms of peace, except such as may be based upon an unconditional surrender of their hostility and a return to their just allegiance to the Constitution and laws of the United States, and that we call upon the Government to maintain this position, and to prosecute the war with the utmost possible vigor to the complete suppression of the rebellion, in full reliance upon the self-sacrificing patriotism, the heroic valor and the undying devotion of the American people to their country and its free institutions.

3. *Resolved,* That as slavery was the cause, and now constitutes the strength, of this rebellion, and as it must be, always and everywhere, hostile to the principles of republican Government, justice and the national safety demand its utter and complete extirpation from the soil of the Republic;—and that while we uphold and maintain the acts and proclamations by which the Government, in its own defence, has aimed a death-blow at this gigantic evil, we are in favor, furthermore, of such an amendment to the Constitution, to be made by the people in conformity with its provisions, as shall terminate and forever prohibit the existence of slavery within the limits or the jurisdiction of the United States.

4. *Resolved,* That the thanks of the American people are due to the soldiers and sailors of the Army and Navy who have periled their lives in defence of their country and in vindication of the honor of its flag; that the nation owes to them some permanent recognition of their patriotism and their valor, and ample and permanent provision for those of their survivors who have received disabling and honorable wounds in the service of the country; and that the memories of those who have fallen in its defence shall be held in grateful and everlasting remembrance.

5. *Resolved,* That we approve and applaud the practical wisdom, the unselfish patriotism, and the unswerving fidelity to the Constitution and the principles of American liberty, with which Abraham Lincoln has discharged, under circumstances of unparalleled difficulty, the great duties and responsibilities of the Presidential office; that we approve and endorse, as demanded by the emergency and essential to the preservation of the nation and as within the provisions of the Constitution, the measures and acts which he has adopted to defend the nation against its open and secret foes; that we approve, especially, the Proclamation of Emancipation, and the employment as Union soldiers of men heretofore held in slavery; and that we have full confidence in his determination to carry these and all other constitutional measures essential to the salvation of the country into full and complete effect.

6. *Resolved,* That we deem it essential to the general welfare that harmony should prevail in the National Councils, and we regard as worthy of public confidence and official trust those only who cordially indorse the principles proclaimed in these resolutions, and which should characterize the administration of the Government.

7. *Resolved,* That the Government owes to all men employed in its armies, without regard to distinction of color, the full protection of the laws of war, and that any violation of these laws, or of the usages of civilized nations in time of war, by the rebels now in arms, should be made the subject of prompt and full redress.

8. *Resolved,* That foreign immigration, which in the past has added so much to the wealth, development of resources and increase of power to this nation—the asylum of the oppressed of all nations—should be fostered and encouraged by a liberal and just policy.

9. *Resolved,* That we are in favor of a speedy construction of the railroad to the Pacific coast.

10. *Resolved,* That the national faith, pledged for the redemption of the public debt, must be kept inviolate, and that for this purpose we recommend economy and rigid responsibility in the public expenditures, and a vigorous and just system of taxation; and that it is the duty of

every loyal State to sustain the credit and promote the use of the national currency.

11. *Resolved*, That we approve the position taken by the Government that the people of the United States can never regard with indifference the attempt of any European Power to overthrow by force or to supplant by fraud the institutions of any republican government on the Western Continent; and that they will view with extreme jealousy, as menacing to the peace and independence of their own country, the efforts of any such Power to obtain new footholds for monarchical governments, sustained by foreign military force, in near proximity to the United States.

CALL FOR THE CONVENTION AT CHICAGO, 1868.

The undersigned, constituting the national committee designated by the convention held at Baltimore, on the 7th of June, 1864, do appoint that a convention of the Union Republican party be held at the city of Chicago, on Wednesday, the 20th day of May next, at 12 o'clock M., for the purpose of nominating candidates for the offices of President and Vice-President of the United States.

Each State in the United States is authorized to be represented in said convention by a number of delegates equal to twice the number of Senators and Representatives to which each State is entitled in the National Congress.

We invite the co-operation of all citizens who rejoice that our great civil war has happily terminated in the discomfiture of rebellion; who would hold fast the unity and integrity of the Republic, and maintain its paramount right to defend to the utmost its existence, whether imperiled by a secret conspiracy or armed force; of an economical administration of the public expenditures; of the complete extirpation of the principles and policy of slavery, and of the speedy reorganization of those States whose governments were destroyed by the rebellion, and the permanent restoration to their proper practical relations with the United States, in accordance with the true principles of a republican government.

MARCUS L. WARD, of New Jersey,
JNO. D. DEFREES, of Indiana, *Secretary*. *Chairman*.

J. B. CLARK, New Hampshire.
A. B. GARDNER, Vermont.
S. A. PURVIANCE, Pennsylvania.
B. C. COOK, Illinois.
D. B. STUBBS, Iowa.
H. C. HOFFMAN, Maryland.
W. J. COWING, Virginia.
C. L. ROBINSON, Florida.
HORACE GREELEY, New York.
B. R. COWEN, Ohio.
N. EDMUNDS, Dakota.
THOS. G. TURNER, Rhode Island.
S. J. BOWEN, District of Columbia.

S. F. HERSEY, Maine.
WM. CLAFLIN, Massachusetts.
J. S. FOWLER, Tennessee.
MARSH GIDDINGS, Michigan.
A. W. CAMPBELL, West Virginia.
N. B. SMITHERS, Delaware.
W. A. PILE, Missouri.
S. JUDD, Wisconsin.
H. H. STARKWEATHER, Conn.
WM. WINDOM, Minnesota.
D. R. GOODLOE, North Carolina.
SAMUEL CRAWFORD, Kansas.
J. P. CHAFFEE, Colorado.

Platform Adopted at Chicago, 1868.

The National Union Republican party of the United States, assembled in National Convention, in the city of Chicago, on the 20th day of May, 1868, make the following declaration of principles:

First. We congratulate the country on the assured success of the reconstruction policy of Congress, as evinced by the adoption, in a majority of the States lately in rebellion, of constitutions securing equal civil and political rights to all, and regard it as the duty of the Government to sustain those constitutions, and to prevent the people of such States from being remitted to a state of anarchy or military rule.

Second. The guarantee by Congress of equal suffrage to all loyal men at the South was demanded by every consideration of public safety, of gratitude, and of justice, and must be maintained; while the question of suffrage in all the loyal States properly belongs to the people of those States.

Third. We denounce all forms of repudiation as a national crime; and national honor requires the payment of the public indebtedness in the utmost good faith to all creditors at home and abroad, not only according to the letter, but the spirit of the laws under which it was contracted.

Fourth. It is due to the labor of the nation that taxation should be equalized and reduced as rapidly as national faith will permit.

Fifth. The national debt, contracted as it has been for the preservation of the Union for all time to come, should be extended over a fair period for redemption, and it is the duty of Congress to reduce the rate of interest thereon whenever it can honestly be done.

Sixth. That the best policy to diminish our burden of debt is to so improve our credit that capitalists will seek to loan us money at lower rates of interest than we now pay, and must continue to pay, so long as repudiation, partial or total, open or covert, is threatened or suspected.

Seventh. The Government of the United States should be administered with the strictest economy; and the corruptions which have been so shamefully nursed and fostered by Andrew Johnson call loudly for radical reform.

Eighth. We profoundly deplore the untimely and tragic death of Abraham Lincoln, and regret the accession of Andrew Johnson to the Presidency, who has acted treacherously to the people who elected him and the cause he was pledged to support; has usurped high legislative and judicial functions; has refused to execute the laws; has used his high office to induce other officers to ignore and violate the laws; has employed his executive powers to render insecure the property, peace, liberty, and life of the citizen; has abused the pardoning power; has denounced the National Legislature as unconstitutional; has persistently and corruptly resisted, by every means in his power, every proper attempt at the reconstruction of the States lately in rebellion; has perverted the public patronage into an engine of wholesale corruption; and has been justly impeached for high crimes and misdemeanors and properly pronounced guilty thereof by the votes of thirty-five Senators.

Ninth. The doctrine of Great Britain and other European powers, that because a man is once a subject, he is always so, must be resisted, at every hazard, by the United States, as a relic of the feudal times, not authorized by the law of nations, and at war with our national honor and independence. Naturalized citizens are entitled to be protected in all their rights of citizenship, as though they were native born; and no citizen of the United States, native or naturalized, must be liable to arrest and imprisonment by any foreign power, for acts done or words spoken in this country; and if so arrested and imprisoned, it is the duty of the Government to interfere in his behalf.

TENTH. Of all who were faithful in the trials of the late war, there were none entitled to more especial honor than the brave soldiers and seamen who endured the hardships of campaign and cruise, and imperiled their lives in the service of the country. The bounties and pensions provided by law for these brave defenders of the nation, are obligations never to be forgotten. The widows and orphans of the gallant dead are the wards of the people—a sacred legacy bequeathed to the nation's protecting care.

ELEVENTH. We highly commend the spirit of magnanimity and forgiveness with which the men who have served the rebellion, but now frankly and honestly co-operate with us in restoring the peace of the country, and reconstructing the Southern State governments upon the basis of impartial justice and equal rights, are received back into the communion of the loyal people; and we favor the removal of the disqualifications and restrictions imposed upon the late rebels in the same measure as the spirit of disloyalty will die out, and as may be consistent with the safety of the loyal people.

TWELFTH. We recognize the great principles laid down in the immortal Declaration of Independence as the true foundation of Democratic government; and we hail with gladness every effort towards making these principles a living reality on every inch of American soil.

THIRTEENTH. Foreign immigration, which, in the past, has added so much to the wealth, development of resources and increase of power to this nation—the asylum of the oppressed of all nations—should be fostered and encouraged by a liberal and just policy.

FOURTEENTH. This convention declares its sympathy with all the oppressed peoples which are struggling for their rights.

CALL FOR THE CONVENTION AT PHILADELPHIA, 1872.

The undersigned, constituting the National Committee designated by the convention held at Chicago on the 20th of May, 1868, hereby call a convention of the Union Republican party at the city of Philadelphia on Wednesday, the 5th day of June next, at 12 o'clock, noon, for the purpose of nominating candidates for the offices of President and Vice-President of the United States.

Each State is authorized to be represented in the convention by delegates equal to twice the number of Senators and Representatives to which it will be entitled in the next National Congress, and each organized Territory is authorized to send two delegates.

In calling this convention, the Committee remind the country that the promises of the Union Republican Convention of 1868 have been fulfilled. The States lately in rebellion have been restored to their former relations to the Government. The laws of the country have been faithfully executed, public faith has been preserved, and the national credit firmly established. Governmental economy has been illustrated by the reduction, at the same time, of the public debt and of taxation; and the funding of the national debt at a lower rate of interest has been successfully inaugurated. The rights of naturalized citizens have been protected by treaties, and immigration encouraged by liberal provisions. The defenders of the Union have been gratefully remembered, and the rights and interests of labor recognized. Laws have been enacted, and are being enforced, for the protection of persons and property in all sections. Equal suffrage has been engrafted on the National Constitution; the privileges and immunities of American citizenship have become a part of the organic law, and a liberal policy has been adopted toward all who engaged in the rebellion. Complications in foreign relations have been adjusted in the interest of peace throughout the world, while the national honor has been maintained. Corruption has been exposed, offenders punished, responsibility enforced, safe-guards established, and now, as heretofore, the Republican party stands pledged to correct all abuses and carry out all reforms necessary to maintain the purity and efficiency of the public service. To continue and firmly establish its fundamental principles, we invite the co-operation of all the citizens of the United States.

WILLIAM CLAFLIN, of Massachusetts,
Chairman.
WILLIAM E. CHANDLER, of New Hampshire,
Secretary.

JOHN A. PETERS, Maine.
LUKE P. POLAND, Vt.
L. B. FRIEZE, R. I.
H. H. STARKWEATHER, Conn.
JAMES GOPSILL, N. J.
WILLIAM H. KEMBLE, Penn.
HOWARD M. JENKINS, Del.
B. R. COWEN, Ohio.
JOHN COBURN, Ind.
C. B. FARWELL, Ill.
ZACHARIAH CHANDLER, Mich.
J. T. AVERILL, Minn.
DAVID ATWOOD, Wis.
GEORGE W. McCRARY, Iowa.
C. C. FULTON, Md.
FRANKLIN STEARNS, Va.
JOHN R. HUBBARD, W. Va.
WILLIAM SLOAN, N. C.

THOMAS W. OSBORN, Fla.
L. C. CARPENTER, S. C.
JOHN H. CALDWELL, Ga.
JAMES P. STOW, Ala.
M. H. SOUTHWORTH, La.
A. C. FISK, Miss.
S. C. POMEROY, Kan.
B. F. RICE, Ark.
JOHN B. CLARK, Mo.
A. A. BURTON, Ky.
HORACE MAYNARD, Tenn.
E. B. TAYLOR, Neb.
JAMES W. NYE, Nevada.
H. W. CORBETT, Oregon.
GEORGE C. GORHAM, Cal.
JOHN B. CHAFFEE, Col.
W. A. BURLEIGH, Dakota.
SAYLES J. BOWEN, D. C.

WASHINGTON, D. C., *January* 11, 1872.

Republican National Committee,
1872.

GEORGE E. SPENCER	Decatur, Alabama.
POWELL CLAYTON	Little Rock, Arkansas.
GEORGE C. GORHAM	San Francisco, California.
MARSHALL JEWELL	Hartford, Connecticut.
JAMES RIDDLE	Wilmington, Delaware.
WILLIAM H. GLEASON	Biscayne, Florida.
ISHAM S. FANNING	Augusta, Georgia.
J. Y. SCAMMON	Chicago, Illinois.
OLIVER P. MORTON	Indianapolis, Indiana.
G. M. DODGE	Council Bluffs, Iowa.
JOHN A. MARTIN	Atchison, Kansas.
WM. CASSIUS GOODLOE	Lexington, Kentucky.
G. CASANAVE	New Orleans, Louisiana.
WM. P. FRYE	Lewiston, Maine.
C. C. FULTON	Baltimore, Maryland.
WM. CLAFLIN	Boston, Massachusetts.
WM. A. HOWARD	Grand Rapids, Michigan.
JOHN T. AVERILL	St. Paul, Minnesota.
O. C. FRENCH	Jackson, Mississippi.
R. T. VAN HORN	Kansas City, Missouri.
E. E. CUNNINGHAM	Plattsmouth, Nebraska.
JAMES W. NYE	Carson City, Nevada.
WM. E. CHANDLER	Concord, New Hampshire.
ALEXANDER G. CATTELL	Camden, New Jersey.
EDWIN D. MORGAN	N. Y. City, New York.
JOSEPH C. ABBOTT	Abbottsburg, North Carolina.
B. R. COWEN	Cincinnati, Ohio.
JOSEPH G. WILSON	Portland, Oregon.
WM. H. KEMBLE	Philadelphia, Pennsylvania.
WM. D. BRAYTON	Warwick, Rhode Island.
FRANKLIN J. MOSES, Jr	Charleston, South Carolina.
HORACE MAYNARD	Knoxville, Tennessee.
EDMUND J. DAVIS	Austin, Texas.
GEORGE NICHOLS	Northfield, Vermont.
H. H. WELLS, Jr	Richmond, Virginia.
HANSON CRISWELL	Moundsville, West Virginia.
DAVID ATWOOD	Madison, Wisconsin.
JOHN TITUS	Tucson, Arizona.
EDWARD M. MCCOOK	Denver, Colorado.
WM. H. H. BEADLE	Dakota.
HENRY D. COOKE	Washington, District of Columbia.
JOHN R. MCBRIDE	Boise City, Idaho.
LUCIUS B. CHURCH	Helena, Montana.
JOSEPH G. PALEN	Santa Fé, New Mexico.
ALFRED S. GOULD	Salt Lake, Utah.
L. B. ANDREWS	Seattle, Washington.
WILLIAM T. JONES	Cheyenne, Wyoming.

REPUBLICAN NATIONAL COMMITTEE.

E. D. MORGAN..*Chairman.*
WM. E. CHANDLER..*Secretary.*

EXECUTIVE COMMITTEE.

E. D. MORGAN..New York city.
WILLIAM CLAFLIN...Boston.
MARSHALL JEWELL...Hartford, Connecticut.
A. G. CATTELL...Merchantville, New Jersey.
OLIVER P. MORTON..Indianapolis.
WM. H. KEMBLE...Philadelphia.
JOHN Y. SCAMMON..Chicago.
B. R. COWEN..[Ohio] Washington, District of Columbia.
GRENVILLE M. DODGE..Council Bluffs, Iowa.
GEORGE E. SPENCER..Decatur, Alabama.
C. C. FULTON..Baltimore, Maryland.
HENRY D. COOKE..Washington, District of Columbia.
JOSEPH C. ABBOTT...Abbottsburg, North Carolina.
GEORGE C. GORHAM.......................................[Cal.] Washington, District of Columbia.
J. T. AVERILL...St. Paul, Minnesota.
WM. A. HOWARD..Detroit, Michigan.

HEADQUARTERS: Fifth Avenue Hotel, New York city.

UNION REPUBLICAN CONGRESSIONAL COMMITTEE.

Eugene Hale	Maine.
Senator Cragin	New Hampshire.
Luke P. Poland	Vermont.
B. T. Eames	Rhode Island.
H. H. Starkweather	Connecticut.
John H. Ketcham	New York.
Geo. A. Halsey	New Jersey.
Senator Cameron	Pennsylvania.
J. H. Platt, Jr.	Virginia.
Senator Pool	North Carolina.
R. H. Whiteley	Georgia.
Senator Spencer	Alabama.
Geo. C. McKee	Mississippi.
J. Hale Sypher	Louisiana.
John Beatty	Ohio.
Horace Maynard	Tennessee.
John Coburn	Indiana.
Senator Logan	Illinois.
Harrison E. Havens	Missouri.
Senator Chandler	Michigan.
Senator Osborn	Florida.
Senator Flanagan	Texas.
Frank W. Palmer	Iowa.
J. W. Hazelton	Wisconsin.
John M. Coghlan	California.
M. H. Dunnell	Minnesota.
Senator Corbett	Oregon.
Senator Pomeroy	Kansas.
Senator Boreman	West Virginia.
Senator Stewart	Nevada.
John Taffe	Nebraska.
Senator Sawyer	South Carolina.
S. Garfielde	Washington Territory.
J. B. Chaffee	Colorado.
R. C. McCormick	Arizona.
W. H. Claggett	Montana.
W. T. Jones	Wyoming.
N. P. Chipman	District of Columbia.

EXECUTIVE COMMITTEE.
Address: Washington, D. C.

Hon. Z. Chandler, *Chairman.*
Hon. S. Cameron.
Hon. J. A. Logan.
Hon. John Pool.
Hon. H. W. Corbett.
Hon. H. H. Starkweather.

Hon. J. H. Ketcham.
Hon. G. A. Halsey.
Hon. John Coburn.
Jas. M. Edmunds, *Secretary.*
Gov. H. D. Cooke, *Treasurer.*

UNION REPUBLICAN RESIDENT COMMITTEE.

Hon. James Harlan, *Chairman.*
Hon. B. R. Cowen.
Gov. H. D. Cooke.

J. M. Edmunds.
Frederick Douglass.
Richard J. Hinton, *Secretary.*

OFFICERS OF REPUBLICAN STATE COMMITTEES, 1872.

ALABAMA........ *Chairman*—R. W. Healey, Montgomery.
      Secretary—J. C. Keffer, Montgomery.
ARKANSAS........ *Chairman*—Powell Clayton, Little Rock.
      Secretary—J. C. Corbin, Little Rock.
CALIFORNIA ...... *Chairman*—Alvinza Hayward, San Francisco.
      Secretary—William Sherman, San Francisco.
CONNECTICUT..... *Chairman*—Bartlett Bent, Middletown.
DELAWARE....... *Chairman*—H. F. Pickels, Wilmington.
      Secretary—John Cameron, Wilmington.
FLORIDA......... *Chairman*—W. J. Purman, Tallahassee.
      Secretary—James W. Johnson, Monticello.
GEORGIA......... *Chairman*—Henry P. Farrow, Atlanta.
      Secretary—Marcus Grant, Atlanta.
ILLINOIS........ *Chairman*—Charles B. Farwell, Chicago.
      Secretary—Daniel Shepard, Chicago.
INDIANA......... *Chairman*—J. W. Foster, Evansville, Vanderberg co.
      Secretary—J. C. Burnett, Indianapolis.
IOWA........... *Chairman*—Geo. C. Tichenor, Des Moines.
      Secretary—...............................
KANSAS......... *Chairman*—D. R. Anthony, Leavenworth.
      Secretary—Jacob Stotler, Emporia.
KENTUCKY....... *Chairman*—John W. Finnell, Louisville.
      Secretary—J. K. Goodloe, Louisville.
LOUISIANA....... *Chairman*—S. B. Packard, New Orleans.
      Secretary—T. W. DeKlyne, New Orleans.
MAINE.......... *Chairman*—James G. Blaine, Augusta.
      Secretary—Zimro A. Smith, Portland.
MARYLAND....... *Chairman*—Andrew W. Dennison, Baltimore.
      Secretary—John McGarigle, Baltimore.

OFFICERS OF STATE COMMITTEES.

MASSACHUSETTS... *Chairman*—George B. Loring, Salem.
Secretary—George S. Merrill, Lawrence.

MICHIGAN....... *Chairman*—S. D. Bingham, Lansing.
Secretary—Schuyler S. Olds, Lansing.

MINNESOTA....... *Chairman*—C. H. Pettil, Minneapolis.
Secretary—R. N. McLaren, St. Paul.

MISSISSIPPI...... *Chairman*—A. Warner, Canton, Madison county.
Secretary—O. C. French, Jackson.

MISSOURI........ *Chairman*—Henry T. Blow, St. Louis.
Secretary—N. M. Harris, St. Louis.

NEBRASKA........ *Chairman*—C. W. Seymour, Nebraska City.
Secretary—Henry A. Newman, Nebraska City.

NEVADA......... *Chairman*—C. C. Batterman, Virginia City.
Secretary—Stephen T. Gage, Virginia City.

NEW HAMPSHIRE.. *Chairman*—E. H. Rollins, Concord.
Secretary—B. F. Prescott, Concord.

NEW JERSEY...... *Chairman*—Geo. A. Halsey, Newark.
Secretary—S. Alpheus Smith, Plainfield.

NEW YORK....... *Chairman*—Alonzo B. Cornell, New York city.
Secretary—John N. Knapp, Auburn.

NORTH CAROLINA.. *Chairman*—Samuel F. Phillips, Raleigh.
Secretary—J. C. L. Harris, Raleigh.

OHIO........... *Chairman*—Charles C. Walcutt, Columbus.
Secretary—Rodney Foos, Columbus.

OREGON......... *Chairman*—C. W. Parrish, Portland.
Secretary—............................

PENNSYLVANIA.... *Chairman*—Russell Errett, Pittsburgh.
Secretary—E. O. Goodrich, Philadelphia.

RHODE ISLAND.... *Chairman*—William A. Pirce, Johnston.
Secretary—Thomas A. Whitman, Anthony.

SOUTH CAROLINA.. *Chairman*—A. J. Ransier, Charleston.
Secretary—E. W. M. Mackey, Charleston.

TENNESSEE....... *Chairman*—Thomas A. Kercheval, Nashville.
Secretary—Abram Smith, Nashville.

OFFICERS OF STATE COMMITTEES.

TEXAS .... *Chairman*—J. G. Tracy, Houston.
      Secretary—James P. Newcomb, Austin.
VERMONT........ *Chairman*—G. G. Benedict, Burlington.
      Secretary—Kittredge Haskins, Brattleboro'.
VIRGINIA........ *Chairman*—W. H. H. Stowell, Halifax C. H.
      Secretary—John W. Woltz, Richmond.
WEST VIRGINIA... *Chairman*—O. G. Scofield, Parkersburg.
      Secretary—C. C. Cole, Parkersburg.
WISCONSIN....... *Chairman*—E. W. Keyes, Madison.
      Secretary—Frank Leland, Elkhorn.

Printed in Dunstable, United Kingdom